Praise for
The Power of Cult Branding

An essential guide for marketing in the 21st century."

—ALAN M. MECKLER,
chairman and CEO, Jupitermedia Corporation

"Ragas and Bueno teach us the real principles of creating a symbiotic loyalty between our customers and our brand. We need to make our customers partners."

—PHIL LEIGH, vice president of
digital media research,
Raymond James & Associates

A masterfully instructive book on what it really takes to build a powerful brand today. It should be required reading for students at the country's top business schools. I recommend it wholeheartedly to entrepreneurs, executives, visionaries, and managers, who should not just read it, but also live by it!"

—EDWARD P. "NED" GRACE III,
managing director, Grace Venture Partners

THE POWER OF
CULT
BRANDING

How 9 Magnetic Brands Turned Customers
into Loyal Followers (and Yours Can, Too!)

MATTHEW W. RAGAS
BOLIVAR J. BUENO

PRIMA VENTURE

An Imprint of Prima Publishing

Published by Prima Publishing, Roseville, California. Member of the Crown Publishing Group, a division of Random House, Inc., New York.

PRIMA VENTURE and colophon are trademarks of Random House, Inc. PRIMA PUBLISHING and colophon are trademarks of Random House, Inc., registered with the United States Patent and Trademark Office.

Interior diagrams by Mike Tanamachi

Library of Congress Cataloging-in-Publication Data
Ragas, Matthew W.
   The power of cult branding : how 9 magnetic brands turned customers into loyal followers (and yours can, too!) / Matthew W. Ragas, Bolivar J. Bueno.
       p.   cm.
   Includes index.
   ISBN 0-7615-3694-9
   1. Brand name products. I. Bueno, Bolivar J. II. Title.
HD69.B7 R34   2002
658.8'27—dc21   2002025818

02 03 04 05 06 HH 10 9 8 7 6 5 4 3 2 1
Printed in the United States of America

First Edition

Visit us online at www.primapublishing.com

To God and our families, friends, and loved ones.
Your love and support are immeasurable.

Contents

Preface

OLD HABITS die hard. Even after living through the dot-com and Web implosions of 2000 and 2001, far too many marketers and entrepreneurs still seem to be in dreamland when it comes to the very important task of brand building. This frustrates the two of us to no end. Did those responsible for marketing and branding learn nothing from the hundreds of venture-backed technology startups that failed over the past twenty-four months?

We scratch our heads and really wonder.

Sure, we may no longer be blowing millions of our clients'— or our own—money on flashy Super Bowl ads and extravagant "launch parties," but many of us still haven't put down the Kool-Aid entirely. We may all talk a good game at industry gatherings about learning great marketing lessons from the recent debacle, but we are an industry that is clearly still in denial.

Many of us are still trying to market our brands like it's 1999.

How do we know this? Because every week we invariably encounter a company either through our consulting work or through scanning the business media that has just announced or is planning to announce plans to launch a massive new advertising campaign. Sometimes the companies making these announcements are small and unestablished, but other times they are entrenched multinational corporations. They all have an itchy trigger finger when it comes to advertising.

Of course, there is nothing wrong with advertising or ad campaigns. On the contrary, we are strong believers that even the most magnetic brand will eventually die a slow and painful death without some form of consistent advertising support. No, it's the comments by these companies' executives and marketing directors explaining why they launch these massive campaigns that really drive us up the wall.

Their rationale can generally be summarized as follows: We're launching this new campaign because we want to "build our brand."

There is nothing wrong with wanting to build your company's brand, either. Brand building is a good thing. What's idiotic about this thinking is that apparently a lot of executives in corporate America and on Madison Avenue still think the most effective (and perhaps the only) way to build a successful magnetic brand is to advertise and advertise and advertise. . . .

After all, if you advertise to death, consumers will eventually have no choice but to fall in love with your brand.

Baloney!

When we see this behavior repeated again and again, it only confirms our belief that brand building is the least understood area in all of marketing. Effective advertising is only one small part of what a company must do to build a magnetic brand and establish lasting customer loyalty.

You don't have to take our word for it. Just look at what happened over the past three years to the majority of dot-com companies that excitedly burned through hundreds of millions of dollars in venture capital on splashy advertising to supposedly "build the brand." If there was ever a group of companies convinced that nonstop traditional advertising was the key to brand building, it had to be these firms.

Surprise! Most of these dot-com companies were dreadfully wrong and are now dead and buried six feet under.

Many suffered from what we call the Revolving Door Syndrome. In other words, these firms paid huge dollars to get their initial customers in the door, but because their product or service produced a lousy or inconsistent brand experience, they lost those customers and had to spend more millions luring new ones. In trying to con the new customers, they neglected the ones they already had. It's not surprising that brand loyalty was virtually nonexistent in the old dot-com land.

While the two of us have always been fascinated with marketing, branding, and customer loyalty, we've both had experiences over the past four years that have really heightened our interest in this area. Having worked or consulted for numerous Internet companies during this time (some big home runs, some flameouts), we began to realize that perhaps the biggest factor in the downfall of the dot-com sector was its lack of brand-loyal fans. We think a loyal cadre of core repeat customers could have saved many a dot-com firm from ruin.

Every sustainable business must have a loyal core group of repeat customers. It's that simple. Build and sustain customer loyalty or die.

Easier said than done, of course. There isn't exactly a blueprint that an entrepreneur or marketer can follow to start turning his or her customers into loyal believers.

While there are dozens of fancy marketing books on bookstore shelves about brand building and customer loyalty, few if any contain the kind of battle-tested and practical advice that we were seeking in this area for our own use. Nor did they offer fresh ideas. Unfortunately, most marketing books have always read to us like the same ideas recycled over and over again. We wanted to find a real guide we could use with our clients and within our own businesses to help create a loyal core of repeat customers.

After multiple trips to the local Barnes & Noble and some caffeine-fueled late-night searching on Amazon.com, we were forced to the conclusion that the battle guide we had envisioned had yet to be written. A realistic book on branding simply didn't exist. To us, this smelled like a sweet opportunity and a huge challenge rolled into one. Add to this the fact that we're both entrepreneurs, both marketers, both writers—and are two individuals not shy about sharing our opinions—and we knew what we had to do. We had a book to write.

The book you're holding in your hands is the product of more than a year of meticulous research and scores of interviews with loyal customers and managers of nine very special modern brands. We worked tirelessly and tried to leave no stone unturned when it came to understanding the secrets to long-lasting brand loyalty. That's why inside these pages you'll find the real behind-the-scenes stories of these nine brands and their fanatical followers, as well as advice on how you can turn your own customers into loyal followers who become walking, talking brand evangelists for your company.

This isn't the kind of book that pulls any punches or tries to hide for safety behind conventional marketing wisdom. Truth be told, we sometimes enjoy making noise in a quiet but crowded room. In fact, if some of the ideas and conclusions that we've reached in this book help to spark debate and controversy within your own company or the marketing and advertising world as a whole, then so be it. We want to make you think. We want you to question the very way you're doing business today and how you plan to do business in the future. If we do that, we've accomplished our job.

Acknowledgments

We have countless people to thank for making this book possible.

For starters, the entire team at Prima Publishing and the Crown Publishing Group has been nothing short of fantastic. We would like to thank everyone from Prima who worked so hard on this book, especially our editor, David Richardson, who believed in us and the power of this project from the very beginning.

Special thanks also goes out to the nine cult brand companies profiled in this book and the many executives and employees of these nine firms who were gracious enough to let us interview them and ask a number of tough and very direct questions about their businesses and marketing practices. This book would simply have been incomplete without their great first-hand insights and experiences.

We were also lucky enough to speak extensively with literally dozens of customers of our nine cult brand companies as part of our research. Thus, we owe a big heartfelt thank you to *every* Trekker, Parrot Head, Harley owner, Oprah fan, Linux user, Mac owner, WWE fan, VW Bug owner, and Vans wearing teenager who spoke to us. Thank you all for very patiently and graciously sharing with us your unbridled passion and excitement for these unique brands!

Of course, we are also extremely grateful to all of our family members, loved-ones, friends, teachers, and colleagues who encouraged us countless times to persevere through this entire process, gave us many tremendous ideas, and were nothing but always accommodating to our deadlines.

You were *and are* our very special *twelfth man*!

And our final thanks go out to you, the reader, for not only buying our book, but traveling with us on this cult branding adventure to marketing lands previously unexplored. We sincerely hope that you enjoy the ride and pick up some powerful new brand-building tactics and customer loyalty ideas along the way.

Finally, don't forget to drop us a line and share with us your own cult branding stories! We always try to respond to all of our e-mails within twenty-four hours (Matt@PowerofCultBranding .com and BJB@PowerofCultBranding.com).

Good luck in all of your future branding battles!

Introduction

Our Search for the Secrets
to Brand Loyalty

Passionate about

W<small>E ARE A</small> society that is absolutely addicted to brands.
We love them. We need them. We surround ourselves
with them.

When they delight us, we build them up. When they disappoint us, we tear them down.

When it comes to our favorite brands, we enjoy telling whoever will listen how great they are and why we love them so much.

Yes, our society has brands on the brain.

Heck, we often judge others—even total strangers on the street—by the brand of car they're driving and the designer label on the clothes they're wearing.

Many of us don't realize the power that brands wield. Yet every single time we buy a product or service, we make a conscious decision to purchase one brand over another. Brands hold more influence over our lives than many of us would care to admit.

This is absolutely the reason every company in the world wants to build a magnetic brand. Brands are spheres of influence, and the most magnetic brands flat out win in the marketplace. They get repeatedly chosen over the competition. They bring higher prices than the competition. And if they're a strong enough brand, their customers not only use their products, but evangelize to the world about them.

There is likely no one reading this book right now that can tell us they wouldn't like to own, control, or work for a company that holds a magnetic brand. Magnetic brands sell more products and make more money than the competition. And isn't that the ultimate goal of every business? To make as much money each year as possible?

Most important though, magnetic brands exhibit a high degree of customer loyalty. Their customers not only choose their product or service over the competition once or twice, but do so week after week, month after month, and year after year. Customers are hooked and happy, and that's what really makes their loyalty such a beautiful thing for businesses. This much devotion gives a brand almost a locked-in cadre of customers who will come back with more business. A core group of happy repeat purchasers. While the companies that make lesser brands constantly struggle to bring in new customers only to churn through most of them, magnetic brands sit back confidently knowing that they always have a built-in customer base.

As students of marketing, we have, not surprisingly, always been fascinated by magnetic brands and what makes them tick, as well as consumer behavior and customer loyalty. About two years ago, after much debate between the two of us, we came to the conclusion that some magnetic brands demonstrate such a high degree of customer loyalty among their customer bases that they deserve to be put into a category all by themselves. They are more than just magnetic brands. They don't just greatly influence purchase decisions, they actually become a crucial part of their customers' lives and actual identity.

One thing led to another, and soon the two of us were reading about the history of cults and infamous cultic groups and leaders. Jonestown and Jim Jones. David Koresh and the Branch Davidians. Marshall Applewhite and Heaven's Gate. Which followers of an organization have ever shown more loyalty, devotion, and attraction to some person or some thing than members of a cult? While there is no commercial product in the world that a person would ever die for, there are very interesting similarities between extreme cults and a special breed of magnetic business brands. It is these brands' super high customer loyalty that we found so fascinating and began to study.

The Difference Between Destructive and Benign Cults

Having done our reading, we combined the two ideas of cultic groups and magnetic brands and found that the combination perfectly described a new, separate class of magnetic brands. These special brands all command super-high customer loyalty and almost evangelical customers or followers who are devoted to them. Because of these characteristics, we decided to call them cult brands. In developing our terminology for this phenomenon, we came up with the term "cult branding" to describe the process of actually turning a company, person, place, or organization into an entity with devoted followers who identify with it and show their commitment in various visible ways. Now, before anyone starts trying to attach the negative aspects of the word "cult" to this approach to marketing, let us briefly explain the very sharp differences between cultic groups and cult brands.

As part of our research, we began talking to numerous cult experts. We were fortunate enough to conduct a detailed interview with Rick Ross, a well-known thought-reform consultant. For over fifteen years, Ross has studied cultic groups and helped rescue family members trapped inside cult compounds. He served as a consultant to the FBI and the bureau of Alcohol, Tobacco and Firearms during the Branch-Davidian stand-off in Waco, Texas. Having seen cults in action, Ross breaks them down into two distinct groups: destructive cults and benign cults.

Ross describes destructive cults as "groups with an absolute authoritarian figure at the top of a pyramid scheme of authority where there is virtually no accountability for that leader."[1] Destructive cults hurt, harm, manipulate, and often brainwash their members. The leader of a destructive cult really doesn't care about the well-being of the members. In fact, such leaders openly exploit and abuse their members, usually for their own personal benefit. Benign cults are a different story. Ross defines these non-injurious cults as "any group of people that are intensely devoted to a person, place, or thing," but where the relationship between the follower and the cult is harmless or benign.[2]

The important thing about benign cults is that they help fill the emotional wants and needs of their followers in a positive way. Benign cults and their followers enjoy a mutually beneficial relationship, with both receiving a real sense of satisfaction, accomplishment, belonging, and enlightenment from the relationship. Benign cults are never destructive. They don't harm or injure their followers either physically or mentally. Benign cults have leaders who are accountable to the group, and the leaders value the feedback of their followers. For the purpose of this book, whenever we discuss cult brands and cult branding, we will always be talking about benign cults.

Cult Branding Won't Work for My Brand and My Customers

Everyone likes to believe they are strong-minded and not easily influenced by others. Nevertheless, the reality is that every human being is readily open to influence in one way or the other. Many of us are influenced every single day by advertisements, a persuasive sales person, or even a friend or family member, and we don't even realize it. Influence happens, and often there's little we can do about it. Even so, we take comfort in telling ourselves that cult members must be weak-minded people or poorly educated or folks that are stupid or crazy or a mixture of both. Of course, this is a classic case of "it won't happen to me" thinking.

Even though millions of people succumb to cult tactics each year, no one likes to think of himself or herself as a victim or—worse yet—a sucker. Instead, we keep telling ourselves that we're far too intelligent and savvy to ever fall for cult persuasion. Cults are for *other people.* While this makes us feel good, it couldn't be further from the truth! Read what Dr. Margaret Singer, arguably the world's foremost expert on cults, has to say. In her book, *Cults in Our Midst,* she reports, "Research indicates that approximately two-thirds of those who have joined cults came from normal, functional families and were demonstrating age-appropriate behavior around the same time they entered a cult."[3]

This finding by Dr. Singer gels exactly with the experiences of cult expert Ross. He told us that his work over the years has demonstrated again and again that cult members "represent a typical cross section of the population." Maybe you still refuse to believe that you and your customers are susceptible to cults, influence by others, and persuasion. That's fine. Look at what a third expert has to say. Jerry Whitfield, a former Scientologist, has worked professionally in the thought-reform field for over a decade, having helped clients on four continents. He painted for us the following picture when we asked him for a short profile of today's typical cult member:

> The general profile of a cult member is a person who has above average intelligence, is open and honest with other people, and anticipates that people will be open and honest back to them. This person has the ability to think in abstract terms and is probably altruistic. They want to help and change things. They want to improve their life and the lives of others. This probably describes almost every fireman in the world.[4]

Now, if Whitfield's profile doesn't sound like a good description of you, your friends, family members, coworkers, or relatives, then we don't know what is! Let us be clear. We don't mean to frighten or alarm you about the power of cults and the influence and persuasion they wield. We included this section in the introduction to demonstrate that many of the ideas and theories we have developed around cult brands and cult branding are genuine and aren't coming from somewhere in left field. Cults good and bad have used them successfully for centuries. It's only now that marketers are starting to implement them with any real frequency in the business world.

In fact, we live in an ideal operating environment for cult branders and cult brands. Today's society is full of fragmentation—from broken families and high divorce rates to increasing violence and rising crime rates. As this fragmentation continues, the basic human need for feelings of security, belonging, and social interaction does not go away. It can't be replaced. We still all want to feel loved by a group. Singer touches perfectly on this topic of fragmentation in our society and the huge opportunity it presents cults for recruiting new adult followers in the following passage from *Cults in Our Midst:*

> Many adults today are overwhelmed by the confusion and apparent coldness of our society: the senseless violence, the rampant homelessness, the lack of meaning, the widespread loss of respect for authority figures, the vast numbers of un-employed and marginalized, the insecurity and instability of the job market, the loss of family communication, the lessen-ing role of the established religions, the failing sense of com-munity or even neighborhood. No less bewildered than the adolescents, many mature adults are finding less and less to hold onto in today's technoculture.[5]

While Singer wrote this section with destructive cults in mind, her evaluations are just as relevant for understanding and ex-plaining why we believe cult brands will become increasingly powerful and important in the marketplace over the next decade. Cult brands aren't just companies with products or services to sell. To many of their followers, they are a living, breathing surrogate family filled with like-minded individuals. They are a support group that just happens to sell products and services. Picture a cult brand in this context, and you'll have a much better understanding of why these brands all have such high customer loyalty and devoted followers.

Think of your own family for a moment. Sure, you'll fight with your parents and siblings sometimes, but chances are you've never entirely broken away from your family for an extended period of time. You need the love, attention, and sense of belonging that they offer you. That's exactly how cult branding works. It isn't rocket science. It builds customer loyalty. It grows sales. Society only helps to accelerate the drivers behind its success. Your customers buy cult brands. They are influenced by cult brands. So, let down your guard for a few hours and start thinking how the branding ideas in this book can recharge and revitalize your own business.

We're confident that the lessons, tips, and advice we share with you will apply to your business, whether it's a mom-and-pop shop or a Global 2000 organization. We'll assume from this point forward that your mind is wide open to new ideas and that you are ready to look at marketing and branding in a whole new light. Let the fun begin. The keys to the Cult Branding Kingdom are within your reach if you choose to grab them!

Meet Mister Maslow—The Father of Cult Branding

The connection between customer loyalty and cult brands is an area that up until now has been filled with lots of questions and relatively few answers. For example, we all know that certain brands enjoy incredible customer loyalty and devotion. And that the most loyal customers of certain brands will do seemingly almost anything to support their cherished brands. But why? Why are certain brands so important and meaningful to some customers that they feel compelled to tell the world about them? What makes them go that extra mile?

Successful brand owners will tell you that a solid grasp of human behavior—what motivates people to do certain things and act certain ways—is at the very core of successful marketing. That is why the research for this book included reading many writings on the topics of human behavior and human motivation. This eventually led to study in the field of humanistic physiology, and particularly the work of the late great psychologist Abraham Maslow.

Chances are that if you've ever taken freshman psychology or consumer behavior or business school classes, you may remember Abraham Maslow and his "Hierarchy of Human Needs."

Maslow postulated that we humans have an ascending order of needs and used a hierarchal pyramid to prioritize them. At the bottom levels of the pyramid are our physiological needs, which include basic things like food, shelter, and clothing that we all need to survive. At progressively higher levels in Maslow's Hierarchy are the needs for safety and security, social interaction, and self-esteem. At the very top is self-actualization, a term Maslow coined to describe the ultimate human need to learn, grow, and reach one's full potential as a person.

His book, *Maslow on Management,* is one of the seminal works about human behavior and motivation in the business world. In it, Maslow describes self-actualization as follows:

> A musician must make music, and an artist must paint, a
> poet must write, if he is to ultimately be at peace with him-
> self. What a man can be, he must be. This need we may call
> self-actualization. . . . It refers to man's desire for self-
> fulfillment, namely to the tendency for him to become actu-
> ally in what he is potentially; to become everything that one
> is capable of becoming.[6]

In other words, we all desire on some level to self-actualize, both to be at peace with ourselves and to try to be the best we can be. As humans, we are drawn to people, places, groups, causes, companies, and, ultimately, *brands* that we believe can help us towards our ultimate goal of self-actualization and total fulfillment.

Why the Hierarchy of Needs Is a Crucial Tool for Branding

Perhaps the most important thing to take away from Maslow's Hierarchy of Human Needs is his theory that all human beings start fulfilling their needs at the bottom levels of the pyramid. In short, we fill our low physiological needs first. Higher needs like safety, esteem, and social interaction basically do not exist at this point. Logically, survival comes first. However, once an individual has satisfied his or her lower level needs, the higher level needs become influential in motivating behavior. As Maslow notes time and time again in his work, "Man is a per-petually wanting animal."[7]

This quick refresher on Maslow and his Hierarchy of Hu-man Needs is important, because many of Maslow's findings lie at the core of what makes companies with cult brands so successful. Maslow's writings break down the underlying drivers of human behavior and decision making. Maslow never mentions the phrase "brand loyalty" in his books, but his Hierarchy of Human Needs and concepts like self-actualization are key to understanding why consumers consistently choose one brand over another and enjoy such strong relationships with them.

Throughout this book, you'll see that the makers of cult brands aren't like mainstream marketers whose focus is largely on selling "feature-benefits" from the bottom of the pyramid to their customers. Rather, cult branders enjoy incredible loyalty because they work hard to connect with their customers at the very highest levels of Maslow's Hierarchy. Cult brand companies all have products and services with great "feature-benefits," but their products and services also fulfill the high-level needs of esteem, social interaction, and self-actualization found at the top of Maslow's pyramid.

So, why is fulfilling higher level needs so integral to building strong customer loyalty? What's the connection, you ask? The answer is, higher level needs influence future human behavior much greater than lower level needs. It is the brands that can fulfill human needs on the higher levels of the hierarchy that become irreplaceable in the mind of the consumer. Remember: That's what customer loyalty is really all about. Being irreplaceable. True customer loyalty is not only about getting a customer to consistently choose your brand over another. It's for that same customer to always believe (and then go tell the world) that your company's brand has no equal!

Seven Golden Rules of Cult Branding

We wanted to put real meat on the bones of our cult branding theories, so we began by spending countless hours reading through hundreds of newspaper and magazine articles about different brands. However, this secondary research, together with information we obtained from the companies, could only tell us so much. To learn more, we began tracking down and speaking with customers and managers of the cult brands we had in mind. Researching this book quickly transformed the two of us into real cult-branding detectives!

We wanted to learn absolutely everything—including the warts and blemishes—about each of these brands from the mouths of their followers. Why do people love this brand? Why are they so loyal to it? What does this brand mean to them? Why? Why? Why! We can't tell you how many times we stopped complete strangers in stores or on the street in the past year when we heard them talking about one of our nine cult brands and interviewed them on the spot. So you've used a Mac for ten years. Why? So you ride a Harley. Why? So you've been to five Buffett concerts. Why? So you love watching *Oprah*. Why? So you just bought a New Beetle. Why?

An interesting thing starts happening after you've asked a lot of questions for a long enough period of time. Not only do you start getting some really good answers, but you begin to see patterns and similarities between the responses that you receive. This was exactly what we saw happen in the dozens of interviews we conducted. Clear patterns emerged. They were the same patterns that emerged from our reading. While each of the nine brands was clearly different, their individual formulas for cult-branding success shared many of the same core ingredients.

We can speak from experience when we say that nothing frustrates us more than to read a book that has good ideas but fails to break them down into bite-sized pieces for the reader to digest and implement. We didn't want this to happen with this book. So, after completing our research and interviews, we sat down and compressed all that we had learned about cult branding into seven key points.

These seven points won't tell you everything there is to know about cult branding, but they will give you a nice overview and practical framework to utilize in your own marketing endeavors. Think of this list as your indispensable "Cult Branding Cliff Notes." Here they are. Read them. Use them!

The Seven Golden Rules of Cult Branding

1. Consumers want to be part of a group that's different.
2. Cult brand inventors show daring and determination.
3. Cult brands sell lifestyles.
4. Listen to the choir and create cult brand evangelists.
5. Cult brands always create customer communities.
6. Cult brands are inclusive.
7. Cult brands promote personal freedom and draw power from their enemies.

As we've said before, we're just students of modern marketing. Experienced students, but students nonetheless. We don't claim to have all of the answers to what makes cult brands really tick. But as far as we know, we've delved further and deeper into the world of cult branding and come up with more answers to the relationship between cult brands and customer loyalty than anyone previously. And we want our readers to test and debate our ideas. You will find that in each chapter of this book we take one of our Seven Golden Rules and explore it in detail for the entire chapter.

Again, we know that talk can be cheap in marketing land, which is why we back up each of our Seven Golden Rules with the actual stories, lessons, and marketing ideas that have and haven't worked for the nine cult brands we studied. Their real triumphs. Their real failures. While no one can always accurately predict the future, there are indeed many lessons that we can all learn from the past. Nine of the world's most powerful cult brand companies are ready to share them in detail with you.

Selecting the Nine Premier Cult Brands

Grand ivory-tower thinking and high level academic theories are annoying to most people. We want to see ideas put into practice, not theories floating around in the clouds. Every person reading this book can probably live without more useless fluff in their heads. After all, grand "cloud theories" designed for a perfect world aren't very useful to marketers and brand builders who have to operate in the real world. That's why this book supports its concepts and ideas with stories and experiences of real cult branders in action. What they did right. What they did wrong. And how your brand can follow in their footsteps.

The cult brands in this book are not necessarily the biggest and most well-known brands, but they are companies with the most fanatical and most loyal customer followings. These are the brands that consistently connect with their customers at the very highest levels of Maslow's Hierarchy of Needs and form deep and lasting emotional bonds with their followers. You'll notice that some well-known multinational brands are missing here. Coca-Cola, Pepsi, Microsoft, Walt Disney, Ford, DELL, and McDonald's did not make the final cut. Big doesn't necessarily equal the best when it comes to customer loyalty. Customer loyalty can't simply be measured by market share or the size of a company's wallet.

While these big companies are all greatly revered brands, none of them invoke the fire and passion in their customers that makes a genuine cult brand. These brands may have some of the world's largest marketing budgets by far, but none of them enjoy customer relationships that reach the highest levels of Maslow's Hierarchy. These companies still have much to learn about cult branding! Also absent from the list are brands that are still unproven and may be only fads. Think of Cabbage Patch dolls, Razor scooters, Swatch watches, and far too many other trendy consumer products to list here right now. A brand has to have been around for at least a decade to make the list of cult brand candidates.

The final requirement for making the list was that the company had to have been started on a shoestring budget. No millions in venture capital, no other "helping hand" to push the company along in its earliest years. The companies we chose are real businesses that had to start at the bottom and fight and claw their way to the top. Not only are they more interesting to learn about, they are also more inspirational for other marketers. None of the nine cult brands were born with silver spoons in their mouths. They clearly prove that any company or any person can become a cult brand if they truly put their heart and mind into it.

The result of this thorough screening process is the very diverse group of nine cult brands we describe below. Each comes from a different part of the business world (from music and media to manufacturing and technology), but all have similar lessons to teach. There may not be a more diverse collection of brands ever having appeared together in one book. All these nine cult brand companies are attention-getting for slightly different reasons. Yet all of them have fanatically loyal followers—not just customers—who have supported these brands for years now.

The Nine Cult Brands

Oprah Winfrey • Is there anyone alive in the world today who doesn't know who Oprah is? Probably not, considering that the *Oprah Winfrey Show* now airs in more than 100 countries around the world and reaches more than 26 million U.S. viewers per day.[8] Oprah just may be the strongest one-person cult brand in the world today. Just the fact that everyone refers to Oprah on a first name basis demonstrates the personal relationships she has been able to form with millions of her viewers over the past fifteen years—even if these relationships do exist largely through a TV screen Like or dislike Oprah, we all feel that we "know her" in some way. The Oprah brand oozes strong emotions and feelings.

How loyal are Oprah's followers? So loyal that Oprah has hosted the highest rated television talk show in TV history for over a decade. Her ratings longevity and dominance is virtually unheard of in the TV world—let alone the talk show business! So loyal that her two-year-old magazine *O: The Oprah Maga-*

zine is the most successful magazine startup in publishing history. So loyal that 8,500 of her followers paid $185 per ticket last year just to hear her speak at one of her four "summits." So loyal that every single monthly selection (over forty-five different books) of Oprah's Book Club since its inception have amazingly leapt onto the bestseller's list![9]

Without a doubt, Oprah has single-handedly taken the concept of turning customers into lasting loyal followers to the next level. And it hasn't gone unnoticed. In 1998, *Time* magazine named Oprah one of the hundred most influential people of the 20th century. *Fortune* magazine estimates that Oprah today controls a "$1 billion empire." The break-away success of this self-described "colored girl from Mississippi" is all the more amazing given that she came from quite humble beginnings (a broken family, child abuse, and a house with no running water).[10] One cannot successfully learn the full power of cult branding without studying the Oprah phenomenon in depth.

The Volkswagen Beetle · How popular has the Beetle been over its more than fifty-year life span? So popular that in 1981 it passed Henry Ford's Model T as the world's best-selling automobile. Over 22 million of the original Beetle has been sold since it first went into mass production in Germany in 1938.[11] Of course, sales and popularity alone do not make a cult brand. What interests us the most about the Beetle is the enduring passion and zeal that people everywhere still have for it. Why is the Bug the world's most loved car?

Even before the release of the New Beetle by Volkswagen in 1998, there were literally hundreds of active Beetle clubs and organizations all around the world dedicated to restoring and driving old Bugs and meeting with other Beetle owners. While the vast majority of other out-of-production cars quickly fade from memory, the Beetle's hold on the passion and enthusiasm of millions of its followers has never waned. Rallies and meets for classic Beetles regularly still attract hundreds of enthusiasts, even though VW stopped importing the original Bug into the U.S. back in 1977. Today, Mexico is one of only four countries that still make the original Bug.

The Beetle also fascinates us because it is a brand that has managed to stay at the top of Maslow's Hierarchy for nearly fifty years. The staying power of the Bug brand cannot be understated. Ownership of a Beetle is just as much a statement of individuality and self-expression today as it was back in the fifties and sixties. How many other brands can we point to that have managed to stay cool for multiple generations? There simply aren't many. The Beetle brand continues to make and maintain strong emotional connections with many of its followers. To understand the strong memories that cult brands create, we couldn't help but study the Bug!

Star Trek · While the original *Star Trek* TV show lasted only a short time, it has spawned one of the most successful television and motion picture franchises in entertainment history. Star Trek seems to age like fine wine. It has spawned five separate televisions series and nine different movies over the past thirty-five years and in the process has become one of the licensing industry's most enduring properties. Star Trek merchandise has generated roughly $2 billion in retail sales since creator Gene Roddenberry had his great idea.[12]

None of this success would have happened without the undying support of the Trekkers, the legions of loyal Star Trek fans that consistently scoop up both new and old merchandise, watch the TV shows, go to the movies, and attend hundreds of Star Trek conventions held around the world each year. The loyalty of the Trekker nation truly amazes us. While there are other TV programs and movie series with a greater number of total fans (*Star Wars* comes to mind), none exude the same level of excitement and passion that Trekkers regularly demonstrate for their brand. NASA even named its first space shuttle *The Enterprise* after receiving 400,000 requests from Star Trek fans!

As you'll see throughout this book, cult brands always establish strong emotional connections with their followers. Few brands do this better than Star Trek. Talk to any Trekker, and you'll quickly find out that Star Trek is much more to them than a TV show or a motion picture. *Star Trek's* storylines reflect many of the feelings, values, and ideals of its followers and mirror the wants and needs of its customers. Of course, lots of brands have tried to mirror customer wants and needs, but they have failed. So, what makes the Star Trek brand work so beautifully? We had to know. We wanted firm answers to these important cult-branding questions and Star Trek seemed like an ideal place to start.

World Wrestling Entertainment • Daring to be different and the willingness to take significant risks are key components of every cult brand. Perhaps no cult brand better epitomizes this philosophy than World Wrestling Entertainment (formerly the World Wrestling Federation). WWE founders Vince and Linda

McMahon have always been risk-takers, and their fans love them for it. While it would be easy to try to brush aside professional wrestling as just some gimmicky side attraction or fad not to be taken seriously or studied by other marketers, the WWE brand has been rock solid for nearly twenty years now. In fact, it easily has the most loyal and devoted fan base of any major entertainment brand we have encountered.

How loyal are the WWE's fans and how large are their numbers? Really loyal and really big. For starters, over 2.5 million people attended the WWE's 350 live events during 2001 alone. The WWE has delivered eighteen consecutive sellouts at Madison Square Garden in New York. WWE television shows like *Raw* are consistently rated the number-one regularly scheduled cable TV program. And unbeknownst to many, the WWE is the largest and most successful Pay-Per-View provider in the world. WWE also has two monthly magazines with a combined circulation of roughly 7.5 million. In addition, three autobiographies by WWE wrestlers have turned into bestsellers.[13]

The voracious appetite that WWE's fans have for "all things WWE" has helped propel the company's market value to over $1 billion in recent years. A truly amazing feat for what started out as a small regional wrestling company. WWE's relentless drive to dare to be different and take significant risks in its business clearly played important roles in the company's evolution into a cult brand. We believe that the WWE brand is filled with cult branding ideas that deserve to be recognized.

Jimmy Buffett · The record industry is notorious for having one-hit wonders and bands that enjoy success for a few years, release one or two popular albums, and then quickly fade into history. This scenario could have easily happened to singer-songwriter Jimmy Buffett. After all, the only Top Ten hit that Buffett ever had happened back in 1977. And his island-inspired music has always been difficult for the record industry to categorize and figure out how to properly promote. Yet over twenty years later, Buffett couldn't be doing any better as an entertainer. Now in his fifties, Buffett has become a one-man cult brand with few equals.

While he doesn't have the promotional benefit of music videos on MTV, and his songs rarely get played on the radio, Buffett regularly finishes each year among the top twenty earners on the concert circuit. An artist without a current mega-hit simply isn't supposed to be able to sell out entire arenas in a matter of minutes. Yet it's safe to say that as long as Buffett continues to tour each summer, he will remain one of the top grossing live acts in the world. Perhaps even more impressive is the fact that his fans (just call them Parrot Heads) collectively spend some $50 million a year on Buffett concert tickets, albums, merchandise, and food at his four Margaritaville restaurants.[14]

Buffett's Parrot Head legions are so loyal that not only do they continue to purchase hundreds of thousands of copies of his albums each year, they have also sent two books he authored right to the top of the bestseller list. In fact, Buffett is only one of six writers ever to reach the top spot on the *New York Times'* fiction and non-fiction bestseller lists. To say that Parrot Heads have a deep love for Buffett is a drastic understatement. Parrot Heads are addicted to the Buffett brand. They can't get enough of it. But why is this? What brings thousands of fans back to Buffett's concerts year after year? We were enchanted by the secrets of the Buffett brand.

Vans Inc. • Founded in 1966 by entrepreneur Paul Van Doren and his partners, the Vans story is a combination of the American dream and David versus Goliath. While Vans footwear may not be familiar to many people over the age of thirty, Vans has enjoyed an incredible lock for decades now on the ten-to-twenty-four-year-old demographic, particularly among skateboarders, BMX bikers, surfers, and participants in other extreme sports that Vans refers to as "Core Sports." Even in the face of constant attacks from tremendously larger multinational rivals like Nike, Reebok, and Adidas, Vans continues to retain its core followers and to find new ways to expand its business and grow its sales.

Today, Vans operates a growing universe of unique lifestyle-branding enterprises, including over 160 retails stores in the U.S. and Europe, nearly a dozen large Vans skateboard parks around the U.S., its own record label (Vans Records), the Vans Warped Tour, and a number of Core Sports events. Add this all up, and Vans has grown over the past thirty-five years from one small struggling retail shop and shoe factory in Anaheim, California, to a powerful and growing cult brand with millions of loyal followers that now generate annual sales of over $340 million.[15]

As we will discuss in detail later, cult brand companies don't simply sell a product or a service, they sell their customers the tools for building and creating unique lifestyles. Few management teams have done as effective a job over the past six years in building a comprehensive lifestyle environment around their brand. How strong a relationship does Vans have with its customers today? So strong that shoe giant Nike, one of the world's largest corporations and over fifty times the size of

Vans, can't gain any meaningful market share in the Core Sports market. Customer loyalty can't just be bought, and the Vans brand is full of good cult-branding tactics.

Apple Computer • How many times over the past decade have technology commentators written off Apple and left the company for dead? To put it simply, this is a brand that its millions of loyal followers love their Macintosh computers too much to ever let it die. As we write this, Apple Computer is as strong and healthy today as a company and a brand as it has been in years. While the pioneering company founded by Steve Jobs and Steve Wozniak in a cramped garage in Silicon Valley in 1977 now controls only 5 percent or so of the worldwide PC market, it retains the most loyal group of customers of any technology company in the world today.[16]

While saturation of the PC market has forced many major tech companies to either merge or leave the PC market all together over the past few years, the incredible customer loyalty among Mac followers keeps Apple sitting pretty. It still cranks out annual sales of over $5 billion.[17] Even as a niche PC player, it still finds itself setting and defining many of the major trends in the computing business. Cult brands are leaders—not followers. At no time in recent memory was this more evident than, after the release of the wildly successful new iMac in 1997, much larger PC companies like Compaq launched their own iMac-looking PCs.

Brand loyalty in the technology world is virtually nonexistent in our opinion. While there are well-known and powerful brands in this sector, notably Microsoft, there is very little true customer passion and excitement surrounding other technology brands. Can you picture a diehard Microsoft user donating time at a local store to show prospective customers how the newest version of Windows works? We don't think so. Yet thousands of Mac users show up at computer stores and other public places all the time, for free, to evangelize about Apple's products and their love of the Mac. That's customer loyalty! Apple has successfully cracked the customer loyalty code for the past twenty years, and our exploration of cult branding wouldn't be complete unless it included Apple Computer.

Linux • Much like Vans Inc., Linux is a David-versus-Goliath story. For those of you not that familiar with Linux, it is a relatively young operating system that was created in 1991 by a twenty-one-year-old Finnish programmer Linus Torvalds.[18] While Linux started out as a small side project and hobby for Torvalds, it has grown over the past decade to become one of the most popular and well-known operating systems in the world. In fact, recent research suggests that Linux now powers 33 percent of all Web servers in the world today, putting its popularity only behind Microsoft's Windows.[19] Want to make computer programmers break out into big smiles and think of you as more than just a "suit?" Just ask them about Linux.

The amazing thing about Linux's growth is that it is a brand and product not even controlled by one company or organization. It never had millions of dollars behind it for marketing and development. The software code that makes up Linux is written entirely by volunteers. Many of the smartest programmers in the world donate their time on an ongoing basis because they love the product so much. They believe in it. Like any good cult brand, Linux helps empower its followers. Unlike Windows,

Linux has been developed under the philosophy of "open source," which allows developers to freely exchange and modify the intellectual property (code) that comprises the system.

Linux is a powerful differentiator and motivator for software developers. Spend some time in the same room with a group of Linux advocates, and you will feel the same sort of electricity and excitement that must have existed among the American colonists during the Revolutionary War. In the minds of Linux followers, they are fighting a revolution for freedom from shoddy software and building a product "for the people, by the people." It is fascinating to watch. While virtually every other product we can think of that has tried to compete directly with Microsoft has failed, all indications are that Linux will continue to increase its market share in coming years. With a decade of history under its belt, Linux is a unique cult brand that we couldn't pass up in this book.

Harley-Davidson · Even though enough business books have been written about Harley to fill an entire library, there was absolutely no way we could write a book on cult branding and not include Harley-Davidson. To us, Harley is without a doubt the largest and most powerful cult brand in the world today. After all, what other brand do you know of that people regularly feel compelled to tattoo on their skin for life? That's customer loyalty! What started out as a small motorcycle manufacturing company in a shed in Milwaukee back in 1903 has evolved into the sole remaining American motorcycle maker, the top worldwide seller of heavyweight motorcycles, and a company with more successful brand extensions than any other brand we know of.[20]

Today, the Harley logo can be found not only on its legendary chrome-covered motorcycles, but on everything from clothing (MotorClothes) like jackets, T-shirts, jeans, and panties to off-beat items like Harley-branded leather toilet seat covers, playing cards, wall clocks, and coffee mugs. HD also operates Harley-Davidson Cafés in New York and Las Vegas. In recent years, HD has partnered with Ford to manufacture the Harley-Davidson Ford F-150 pickup truck that has sold like hot cakes among Harley enthusiasts.[21] The Hog nation just can't get enough of anything and everything HD. In spite of the fact that Harley has continued to ramp the production of its bikes each year, waiting lists to buy new Harleys are still commonplace at many Harley dealerships around the country.

The undying brand loyalty Harley's followers have for the company became perhaps most apparent in the past two years during the bitter economic recession when Harley's sales continued to soar. The stock market now values Harley's business at a princely $16 billion. *Forbes* magazine recently named HD its Company of the Year.[22] It's hard to believe that this is the same company that nearly disappeared into bankruptcy in the mid-eighties. The lessons for marketers and business people to take away from Harley-Davidson could easily take up two or three hundred pages. However, we will concentrate primarily on exploring HD's incredibly successful creation of its lively "customer communities."

Consumers Want to Be Part of a Group That's Different

M ODERN CIVILIZATION is built upon communication. Think about it. Without communication, we might still all be sitting around the fire in loin cloths, planning the design for our next cave picture.

The human species has an inherent need and desire to communicate. We need to talk to others. We need to learn. We need to express and share our thoughts, feelings, experiences, and emotions with friends and family. Isolation is definitely not our cup of tea. Think of the millions of man-hours the human race has spent on inventing better ways to communicate. The Gutenberg press. The telegraph. The telephone. Fax machines. Pagers. Cellular phones. The Internet. E-mail.

We are addicted to communication because we are social creatures. We like to interact with others. Not only that. When we find other individuals who share our goals or beliefs, we form groups. Virtually every higher-order species in the world also travels or lives in distinct groups. A school of fish. A herd of buffalo. A flock of birds. You get the idea. Animals form groups as a matter of survival, because there is power in numbers. It's unify or perish. Amongst humans, while survival is also a motivator behind communication, we love groups because *we're all social animals and need to be with each other.* The more we have in common, the more we like it.

That's right. Every single one of us is a social animal who has an inherent need to communicate with other people and form groups. We're all blabbermouths! We absolutely hate being isolated either physically or mentally. Being alone kills our spirit and crushes our dreams. Over time, isolation arguably even erodes our identity as individuals. Ask any prison guard what's the surest way to mentally break down even the toughest criminal, and they will all give the same answer: solitary confinement. A man locked in a cell with no input from the outside world is a man who no longer has an identity. He becomes an object, not a person. Human beings don't like feeling alone.

To fight our battle against isolation, we surround ourselves with family, friends, supporters, and like-minded individuals. These people build our confidence. They help us grow. They make us happy. In effect, we all look (often subconsciously) for ways to create *shields of support* in our lives.

Successful entrepreneurs understand this. They create cult brands that attract admirers who not only buy their product or service but who enjoy it so much they form themselves into support groups around it. Suddenly, anonymous buyers have identity. They even give themselves special names. Trekkers. Parrot Heads. Mac users. Harley owners. Volkswagen Beetle enthusiasts. WWE wrestling fans. Even Linux developers and the open-source software community fit this identity mold.

Makers of cult brands, in effect, become much more than manufacturers of a product or providers of a service. They are developers of customer communities. They provide their customers with unique identities. They dare to be different. They sell a lifestyle not just a product. Perhaps most important, the product or service sinks into public consciousness as a tool for the self-actualization described by Abraham Maslow and for temporary escapism. When you wrap all this together, you see how cult brands become symbols for distinct social groups that are recognizably unique and stand apart from society as a whole.

Consumers Aren't Islands unto Themselves

In the down-to-earth words of well-known cult expert and intervention specialist Rick Ross, cult brands effectively give each of their customers a unique way "to be weird together and then feel weird no more." That's why realizing that consumers *don't* just want to live on islands unto themselves is the first major step you'll want to follow to get your own company on the track to increased customer loyalty. Start thinking about how your product can be truly unique and different from that of your competitors. Now, does your brand already stand out from the pack, or is it still chained to the rigid walls of the status quo?

 We are a society addicted to communication. Twenty-four-hour cable news channels. Pagers. Cell phones. E-mail. All in the name of forming and maintaining social groups. Focus your brand on selling to social animals rather than imaginary customer profiles and research projections!

Cult Brands Create Surrogate Families

Today, we find ourselves living in a world well suited for the warmth, support, and uniqueness that cult brands nurture and disseminate to their followers. A land where now more than ever before cult branders and their brands are poised to be kings.

Don't believe it? Well, just consider the pain many of us now face in our daily lives. Divorce rates are rising. Broken homes are frequent. Ads for depression medications are all over our TVs. School shootings are now fact, not just fiction in some scary movie. The prison population is larger than ever. Economically, the workweek is now longer for many, and achieving the American dream still seems always a step or two out of reach. To top it all off, thanks to the wonders of mass production and automation, bland cookie-cutter-looking houses, cars, and clothes are everywhere in our society.

Cult brands may be just what the doctor ordered to ease many of these societal pains. They are a temporary way for consumers to rebel against the plainness of Cookie Cutter, U.S.A., while receiving the much needed support, love, and acceptance of like-minded individuals in the process. Cult brands help fill voids and close the gaps between what people *need* and what they really *want* out of their lives. In effect, cult brands have evolved into launching pads for the creation of distinct social groups of customers that together help serve the purpose of a surrogate family. Interestingly, followers of every cult brand, either by the manufacturer's own doing or by customers' initiatives, regularly congregate in person.

Much like a family, buyers of cult brands enjoy getting together to break bread and swap tales. For Trekkers, this often means meeting on the weekends at any one of thousands of fan-created Star Trek conventions held around the world. "So many Star Trek fans are people who want to belong to a group. That's why they go to these conventions, wear these costumes, and buy all this stuff," says Dan Madsen, founder of the Official Star Trek Fan Club.[1]

Jeff Greenwald, author of *Future Perfect: How Star Trek Conquered Planet Earth,* shares a similar viewpoint on the appeal of Star Trek and cult brands in general. "I think Star Trek, like every brand loyalty enterprise, is a club. They want to be seen as being set apart and having their own noble way of life."[2]

Oprah's Book Club:
A Surrogate Mother and Family in Action

Talk show host Oprah Winfrey may be the greatest wizard of all in helping her customers (the millions of TV viewers of her show) feel not only like one big family but unique individuals at the same time. Oprah has always had a knack for helping her viewers truly feel special and better about themselves and their daily lives. She had this in mind in 1996 when she launched her book club to, as she put it, "help get America reading again."[3] Not only does Oprah personally select the books each month for the club, she also discusses them with her show's audience and invites each author to appear as a guest.

Typically, most media pundits initially viewed Oprah's Book Club as a crazy idea and delusional. They thought talk show viewers didn't seem a likely mix with books. Oprah went ahead anyway. Her monthly selections ignored light and fluffy romance novels and concentrated on literary works dealing with strong emotional conflicts. The formula worked. Oprah's viewers took to the book club idea immediately, so much so that only a year after its launch, *U.S. News & World Report* wrote that Oprah had "set millions to reading who hadn't read a book since high school and has made obscure books bestsellers."[4]

Five years after the club's launch, the placement of the Oprah Book Club logo on a book is the most surefire way for it to rocket onto the bestseller list. Bookstores have so much faith in the "Oprah Effect" that, sight unseen, they happily order each month thousands of copies of her upcoming club selection.

While one can point to a variety of reasons why Oprah's Book Club has been such a huge success, no one can ignore the fact that by participating in this club, *every* Oprah viewer becomes part of the Oprah family for a few hours each week, while still remaining unique from the world's non-Oprah viewers.

"What she brought with the Book Club was this appetite people had out there to feel that they were engaging in something intellectually stimulating," explains Syracuse University professor and popular television expert Dr. Robert Thompson. "Oprah acknowledges that you're different and you're unique, but at the same time she embraces you into this larger family of Oprah."[5]

In early April of 2002, Oprah shocked her millions of fans and the entire publishing world by announcing that she would no longer devote regular broadcasts to her Book Club. The surprise announcement hit the publishing world like a ton of bricks. After all, Oprah's powerful endorsements had become a huge boon to overall book sales over the past five years. As Carolyn Reidy, president of adult publishing at Simon & Schuster, explained to the *New York Times* upon hearing this news,

"There has never been any single person or outlet that has been able to affect book sales in this way."[6]

While Oprah hinted that she would still occasionally recommend some books on her daily show, she explained that it had become increasingly difficult to regularly find books that she felt "absolutely compelled to share." While media critics argued over why exactly Oprah had decided to curtail her Book Club, one thing was abundantly clear: Oprah loved her Book Club, but was ready for a *new* challenge and a *new* way to regularly delight and surprise her loyal audience. Even a $1 billion personal empire still clearly hadn't stopped Oprah from wanting to continue to dare to be different.

Within only a few days of Oprah's announcement, national newspaper *USA Today* and NBC morning show, *The Today Show,* had both announced plans to launch their own book clubs. This *USA Today* and NBC news was yet another blatant example of a group of lagging cult brand competitors desperately trying to play a game of "follow the leader" where the cult brand (Oprah) wrote and controlled all of the rules. One can only wonder what innovative new idea Oprah will introduce to her fans through her show or magazine.

Think about your own brand for a few moments. Does your company already understand that consumers all want to be part of a group that's different? Do your products, services, and employees evoke feelings of support, warmth, and uniqueness? They should! For Oprah, creating a book club was a great way to nurture her surrogate family and help them feel unique at the same time. You too can develop a similar feeling of exclusivity for your customers. Every business large or small can create its own club-like programs and events that reward its best customers.

Changes in society have cult brands poised to be kings. Cult brands nurture and disseminate feelings that relieve some of the pain in our lives. What can *your brand do* to become a surrogate family for your customers? Think hard. Your product holds the answer.

Look, Say, and *Feel:* The Three Amigos of Every Cult Brand

Each and every one of us uses our five senses of taste, touch, smell, sight, and sound countless times each day to gather data and make decisions. The data we gather through our senses help us decide everything from how warm the water should be in the shower in the morning to when it's safe to back the car out of the driveway or walk across the street. In the same way, we use our senses to help us decide which brand of a particular product or service we should or should not buy. Whether we

---

RULE 1: Consumers Want to Be Part of a Group That's Different

Cult Brand Inc.	Others Inc.
Do you want to be different? Do you enjoy being an individual and standing out in a crowd?	What is your yearly income? (If less than $300,000, please do not apply.)
Do you want to be happy? Do you like products that make you feel happy?	Are you in perfect shape and physically fit? (If overweight, please do not apply.)
Do you want to feel loved, appreciated, and welcome among like-minded individuals?	What is your completed level of education? (If no college degree, please do not apply.)
Then, welcome to our family!	**Only ideal customers wanted!**

The entrepreneurs behind cult brands realize that consumers all want to be part of a group that's different and that accepts them for who they *really are*. The world can be a *cold* place. Cult brands are *warm*. Cult Branders don't build barriers and search only for "ideal customers." In short, they make *all* their customers feel loved, welcome, and appreciated!

realize it or not, we sense that every single brand has its own *look, say,* and *feel.*

Not only does each company's brand have its own "look, say, and feel," but more important, each company actually *controls to a large extent* the creation and development of these three variables. No doubt about it, you control how your product or service *looks,* you control what your advertising messages *say,* you even greatly influence what emotions your customers will *feel* about your product. However one cuts it, you, its maker, control your brand's look, say, and feel. Once a company understands this, its brand is ready to wield (and can wield!) significant power in the marketplace.

Almost all makers of cult brands do everything in their control to use the three powerful amigos of *look, say,* and *feel* each and every day to help differentiate their products and services from other offerings on the market. By continually dialing and turning these three look, say, and feel "knobs," so to speak (a little to the right there, a little to the left here), cult branders are able to become and stay standard bearers for products and services that really are unique and different.

The Macintosh Story: *Look, Say,* and *Feel* Up Close

Apple Computer, for one, has always used look, say, and feel as a way to maintain its cult niche in the computing world. While most tech companies spend the majority of their time blindly stumbling in the dark trying to discover and build customer loyalty, Apple has found the matches it needs to continually light new cult-branding fires—and that's just what it does. Even today, to borrow a few legendary phrases from Apple founder and CEO Steve Jobs, Apple strives to "sweat the details" and build "aesthetically beautiful" products that are always "insanely great."

This rigid attention to detail, beauty, and greatness definitely isn't lost on Apple's cult followers. "I like Apple's attention to style and detail. They really try to make the computing process easier," says Apple-History.com founder Glen Sanford. "There are still a lot of things wrong with PCs, but Apple helps overcome them."[7]

Apple's unveiling of the original Macintosh computer in 1984 was *look, say,* and *feel* mastery at its best. The Mac wasn't just different; it was DIFFERENT in capital letters! Here was a product that represented the first major commercial unveiling of a computer that actually had a graphical user interface, point-and-click icons, and a mouse for navigation. These design changes represented quantum improvements for an until-then largely text-based computer world. Yet Apple didn't just stop with the design (*look*) of its computer as a way to build its cult following. It also stressed *say* and *feel* with its initial Mac ads.

Few of us will probably ever forget Apple's famed "1984" television ad to introduce the Macintosh. Directed by Ridley Scott of *Bladerunner* fame, the ad aired only once nationwide during half time of that year's Super Bowl, but it left a lasting impression on millions of viewers for years afterward. In fact, "1984" was eventually named TV Commercial of the Decade by *Advertising Age* magazine. The imagery of "1984" featured a Mac-clad, hammer-wielding female runner battling a totalitarian Big Brother society that was obviously a buttoned-down IBM. The ad positioned Apple as the only symbol of self-empowerment and freedom in personal computing.

"Apple was really the first technology company to ever talk about empowering the individual. That's why we called it the computer for the rest of us," recalls former Apple chief John Sculley. "There's almost a tribal community to Apple's world."[8]

Now, fast-forward to the late 1990s. By this time, Apple's market share in the PC business had significantly eroded, and many industry pundits were leaving the company for dead. Wrong! In early 1998, Apple went back into its bag of *look, say,* and *feel* tricks and unveiled the iMac, an affordable, all-in-one PC inside a funky, translucent plastic case. Mac fans and critics alike all had to admit that the iMac at the very least *looked fun and friendly.* Instead of the standard beige color of other PCs, the iMacs were available in such eccentric shades as grape, strawberry, lime, and even tangerine.

With the iMac's introduction, much as with the Macintosh over a decade before, Apple focused its efforts on complete *look, say,* and *feel* differentiation. Not surprisingly, Apple's new marketing slogan became two simple but very powerful words: "Think Different." This new slogan appeared in marketing campaigns featuring black-and-white imagery of highly identifiable figures like Einstein, Picasso, Churchill, and Gandhi.[9] Again, Apple was back selling to consumers the fact that not only were its products uniquely designed, they all spoke the common language of freedom of the individual and

---

 Cult brands often achieve and maintain differentiation of their brands through look, say, and feel. So, does your product look unique? What does your brand say? What do customers of your brand feel? Do you really know? Get honest answers to all three of these questions.

---

the freedom of the computer user. In other words, self-empowerment at its best.[10]

With over six million machines sold, the iMac is now one of the best-selling PC lines of all time.

The Volkswagen Story:
The Little Car That Conquered the World

The astonishing rise of the Volkswagen Beetle from virtual unknown to the little car that conquered the world is another great example of *look, say,* and *feel* and brand building at its best. Virtually everything about the original Beetle's design screamed that it was a car like no other. To begin with, its small air-cooled engine was mounted *in the back,* not the front like every domestic gas guzzler of the period. In addition, due to the Beetle's unique rear-engine configuration, the trusty little car was more adept than any U.S.-made car of the time for safe driving in rain, sleet, and snow.

Perhaps the greatest difference between the Beetle and other cars of the 1950s and 1960s was the Beetle's incredibly unique exterior design. The Beetle's rounded, almost egg-shaped body stood in sharp contrast to the large and sleek, chrome-covered domestic behemoths of the period. The Beetle's unique appearance seemed to ooze a curious combination of personality and practicality, which helped quickly build strong affection for it among its owners.

"If there ever was a car that lent itself to personification, it was the Beetle. If you look at the front of the car, it has a face. It has this innocent little look to it," says Beetle aficionado and *Bug Tales* author Paul Klebahn.[11]

In addition to its unique design elements (the *look*), Volkswagen, much as Apple did later with the Macintosh, also focused on developing a unique marketing message (the *say* and *feel*) for the Beetle. While the advertising of the Detroit automakers of the 1960s (and today for that matter) was full of slick copy and boastful claims, VW's Beetle ads from the late fifties onward were always refreshingly frank, direct, and honest with car buyers. In other words, Beetle ads were almost the exact *opposite* of the typical car ad. Some of the more memorable early VW print ads included "Think small," "Some shapes are hard to improve on," and the cult-branding clincher, "Do you earn too much to afford one?"[12]

The Beetle's unique design elements and honest, sometimes even self-deprecating advertising became a killer combination. By the early 1960s, this funny looking economy car had become a magnet for legions of Americans who saw themselves as being different. Think rebels with a car—*and a cause. Bug Tales* author Paul Klebahn nicely sums up this counter-culture sentiment surrounding early Beetle owners. "The Beetle tended to appeal to freethinkers. This was the thinking person's car. Instead of saying, look how much I paid for my car, it was look how much I *didn't* pay!"[13]

For dyed-in-the-wool Beetle lovers, VW's winning formula of having a distinct *look, say,* and *feel* for its original Beetle as well as for the New Beetle released in 1998 hardly seems surprising—to them, it's just common sense. "The Beetle has always been unique," says David Allen, organizer of the annual Roswell 2K New Beetle show, one of the largest of its kind in the U.S. "People like to be different." Indeed they do, and because of this inherent human need, the Beetle has gone on to become the greatest selling car of all time, or as Allen puts it, "the underdog car that conquered the world!"[14]

 Early critics of the Beetle called the odd little egg-shaped car an "ugly duckling." But time has proved all these critics wrong. As the best-selling car in history, the Beetle was really just a beautiful swan in hiding. Think like an underdog. Embrace your brand's differences!

Little Things Can Make a Big Difference

Makers of cult brands don't just focus on painting *look, say,* and *feel* onto their canvas with big bold brush strokes. In fact, if anything, makers of cult brands are all addicted to details. From Apple's Mac and Volkswagen's Beetle to Jimmy Buffett and World Wrestling Entertainment, *each and every one of these makers of cult brands* always sweats the small stuff. They just wouldn't have it any other way. Small is big.

The creation and selection of the original Linux logo and mascot is a perfect case in point. By early 1996, lively discussion had begun among open-source developers on the Linux kernel discussion list (a kernel is the core of a program) that the new operating system clearly needed to have its own mascot and logo. Linux needed a recognizable identity. Ferocious animals like sharks, eagles, hawks, and foxes all came up as possibilities. Soon thereafter, though, Linux founder Linus Torvalds hopped into the discussion and casually said to the open-source community that he was rather fond of penguins. Why was Linus a penguin fan? Simple. They were in his words "cute" and "cuddly."[15]

Last time we checked, "cute" and "cuddly" are hardly the feelings one gets from viewing the logos of other tech products. Cold and corporate is more like it. That's why a fun-loving penguin was the perfect match for upstart Linux and its anti-command, anti-control mentality. It screamed: We're different! But Linus Torvalds didn't just want any old penguin for the Linux logo. He wanted one that "looked happy, as if it had just polished off a pitcher of beer and then had the best sex of its life," as David Diamond noted in the book *Just for Fun,* which he co-authored with Torvalds.[16]

After Linus spoke his mind and the Linux community decided upon a penguin as its official logo, an informal contest was held to select the exact penguin logo that Linux developers could rally behind. The eventual choice was a fun painting of a plump but content sitting penguin submitted by graphic artist Larry Ewing.

"All the other logos were too boring. I wasn't looking for the Linux Corporate Image. I was looking for something fun and sympathetic to associate with Linux. A slightly fat penguin that sits down after having a great meal fit the bill perfectly," explained Torvalds in a Web posting later on the topic.[17]

Today, the Linux Penguin logo appears in everything from IBM's high-profile TV and print ad campaigns promoting the Linux operating system to Linux T-shirts, toys, and product packaging. In fact, the open-source community has even given the plump penguin its own name, Tux. The imaginary penguin is truly a star. So, sweat the details with your own product or service. It's the little things that can blossom almost overnight into the big things that really separate your brand from the competition. Don't be afraid to be different in everything that your brand does. Even if it's the seemingly small stuff. Remember the story of Tux the Penguin!

 Perhaps it's too late for you to change your company's logo. This doesn't mean you can't have some fun with your brand. What's the worst thing that could happen? Your customers might just think that you're fun, easy to work with, and *not* just a faceless corporate entity.

Maximize Your Brand's Differences: Create a Category

Oprah's Book Club, the Apple Macintosh, the VW Beetle, and Tux the Penguin are all great examples of how companies go about satisfying our human need to form unique social groups. Yet this chapter wouldn't be complete without the tale of a cult brand with a unique *look, say,* and *feel* that just wouldn't quit. You guessed it. The non-quitter is "Mr. Magaritaville" himself, the perennial singer/songwriter Jimmy Buffett.

Today, Jimmy Buffett is widely regarded as one of the world's top performers and a killer cult brand, earning millions of dollars per year peddling his unforgettable island medleys. Yet thirty-odd years ago, Jimmy Buffett was a young nobody musician from sleepy Mobile, Alabama. Upon graduating from college in 1969, Buffett moved to Nashville to take his shot at making it big in the music business. The Music City did not embrace him with open arms. In fact, as legend has it, over twenty record labels rejected Buffett's advances!

Finally, after two years of writing for *Billboard* magazine in Nashville, Buffett found a home for his music with Barnaby Records, a Columbia Records label. Buffett's first album, *Down to Earth,* was hardly a hit, though. As author Mark Humphrey notes in *The Jimmy Buffett Scrap Book,* "Legend has it *Down to Earth* sold a grand total of 374 copies."[18] This flop would have marked the end for most musicians, but Buffett pressed onward and was able to land a new record deal with ABC/Dunhill in 1973.

Buffett methodically churned out new albums for ABC over the next few years, but he wasn't raking in the dough or producing any chart-topping hits. If anything, Buffett's unique blend of lively country and folk music with a Caribbean sound left his record company and the entire music industry confused about how to properly market him. Jimmy Buffett's musical sound was truly in a category unto itself, and he fought hard to keep it that way.

"He didn't try to pigeonhole himself, even though the music industry did. One of the reasons that he had a problem getting his music out there initially is that he couldn't be categorized," recalls Buffett fan and Margaritaville Inc. veteran Cindy Thompson. "There really isn't a way to put a finger on his kind of music."[19]

It wasn't until 1977 and the release of the beach song "Margaritaville" from Buffett's sixth album that he finally enjoyed his first (and what has been his only) Top Ten hit. But the wait was well worth it. Almost twenty-five years later, anything even remotely sounding like "Margaritaville" by another artist is still invariably referred to as "Jimmy Buffett music." Buffett effectively "owns" his own category of music in the minds of millions. In the retailing world, the Buffett brand would undoubtedly be referred to as a "category killer."

While it surely would have been easy for Buffett to give in to the record label execs and try to sound like just another country or folk musician, Buffett's stubbornness and persistence paid off. Big time. Every brand has the opportunity to eventually become a category killer just like Buffett, if they're willing to step out onto the ledge, withstand the initial criticism, and stay there. Refuse to let your brand be pigeonholed. Relish looking and sounding different. While this strategy isn't for everyone, if you're serious about getting attention in the marketplace and attracting loyal followers and keeping them, then the Buffett game plan should always be on your mind.

Want to really turn your industry on its head? Then blaze a new trail. Step far out onto the ledge and stay there. Create a new category for your brand. Become a category killer. Take a chance! Brands that resist being pigeonholed become cult brands that command attention.

A Cult Brand Is Insanely Different

Start viewing your company's brand through the eyes of your customer for at least a few minutes each day. Become a social animal and not a marketer for a little while. Shop—don't sell. What do you see when you step back? You should see a world that looks different from your usual view as a businessperson or storeowner. As social animals, consumers aren't concerned about balance sheets, payroll taxes, or marketing budgets. What they care about each day is communicating with like-minded individuals and identifying distinct brands that speak to their seemingly unique needs and wants.

Under this context, companies that truly want to develop into cult brands must start out with a product that is not only noticeably *different from the competition* but seemingly has no equal. In the mind of a social animal, there can be no substitute for your brand. It must immediately stand alone in a class by itself. In fact, *insanely different* might be the best way to describe how the public should ultimately see your brand. A cult brand follower must believe that absolutely no other product or service can even come close to offering up the same radical mix of *look, say,* and *feel* as their cherished cult brand.

For example, have you ever seen a Harley-Davidson owner dreaming of owning a Japanese motorcycle? Similarly, a Vans-wearing teen laughs at the suggestion of putting on a pair of Nikes, and a Linux developer would rather die than donate time to a Microsoft Windows project. This same story essentially repeats itself over and over again for every cult brand and its followers. They remain hooked and loyal to a particular brand because in their minds there is no substitute or worthy equal in the marketplace. Their cult brand stands alone. Any alternative appears to be woefully inferior.

Nevertheless, cult brands can stumble, fall, stop daring to be different, and lose their cult status. Many have and many will in the future. But cult brands like Jimmy Buffett, Apple Computer, Volkswagen Beetle, and Harley-Davidson have maintained their status for decades because they continue to find new ways to look and act *insanely different* from the competition. Not only do they actively promote a platform for creating customer communities and encouraging feelings of support, they aren't afraid to continually move in the opposite direction from the competition. When the marketplace gravitates to the left, they head right and vice versa.

The fact remains that as humans we can't help but pay attention to things that are different and out of the ordinary. After all, who doesn't glance at a seven-foot-tall basketball player or a guy with a red Mohawk and tattoos? We are drawn to what's insanely different, and savvy makers of cult brands capitalize on this behavior. Look closely at your own brand's product. If tomorrow you took a competitor's product and slapped your logo on it, would your customers really notice the difference? Would your customers perceive a competitor's product to be a worthy substitute for your own? Let's hope not. Cult followers unequivocally believe a cult brand has no close equal.

"My brand is superior." "My brand is superior." Say this again and again until you really believe it and mean it. Then go out and scream from the mountaintop of your marketplace: "My brand is insanely different! It is unique and powerful! It has no substitute! It stands alone!"

Cult Brand Inventors Show Daring and Determination

HISTORY REMEMBERS those individuals who achieved what people once thought was impossible. The dreamers who dared to be different and succeeded. Thomas Edison and the light bulb. Alexander Graham Bell and the telephone. The Wright brothers and the airplane. All of these famous inventors were determined and courageous people who had a seemingly impossible idea and made it work.

The creators of cult brands are like famous inventors. Consumers embrace cult brands and are loyal to them because their creators pushed the limit, took significant risks, and produced new and different things. We admire courage and determination. At the end of the day, no one remembers the naysayers, the people who once said, "Man will never fly" or "Man will never talk across the ocean." Cult brands stay with us. Bland brands fade from our collective memory.

As consumers, we are tired of being bombarded with products and services that all look the same, feel the same, and act the same. Give us something different for a change—not just another big scoop of "the ordinary." We want surprises. We want breaks from the ordinary. We want more than we expected. The makers of cult brands understand this point of view and provide us with much needed breaths of fresh air in a world filled with bland-brand smog.

Look inside your own company for a second. In addition to passion and enthusiasm, does your staff have determination and courage as well? Let's hope so. After all, anyone can dare to be different, but only the determined and the courageous actually have the guts to see the seemingly "impossible" through. Like successful inventors, cult brand holders don't just *dare to be different;* they *are different.* Courage and determination are deep in their hearts.

 The creators of cult brands are like famous inventors. They have the courage and determination needed to dare to be different and succeed. They turn the impossible into the possible. How can you surprise your own customers? How can you give them more than they ever expected?

Don't Just Challenge Conventional Wisdom: Shatter It!

At its core, daring to be different means relentlessly challenging conventional wisdom. Challenge conventional wisdom within your company. Challenge conventional wisdom within your industry. Challenge what conventional wisdom says about your product. Last, but certainly not least, challenge what conventional wisdom says your customers need and want. Never accept a situation because that's "the way it's always been." Unless you want your brand to be bland, boring, and predictable, you're not likely to find any real usable "wisdom" in conventional thinking.

Star Trek is one cult brand that challenged and then repeatedly shattered conventional wisdom. Before the arrival of the original *Star Trek* series in 1967, conventional wisdom among Hollywood executives held that the American TV public *wasn't interested* in watching serious "adult science fiction." However, the loyal following that the original *Star Trek* series quickly won among traditional science-fiction fans proved this notion terribly wrong. In fact, *Star Trek* fans loved the show because it had *real plot lines, real characters*, and *real subject matter.*

"Why I liked *Star Trek* originally was that I already read science fiction books, and *Star Trek* was really the first good serious science fiction on TV," says Sue Cornwell, a thirty-five-year *Star Trek* fan and co-owner of Intergalactic Trading, a sci-fi collectibles company. "They really took the show and the subject matter seriously. They took a subject that no one else took seriously and did it."[1]

Star Trek took its subject matter so seriously that, according to an early promotional booklet, the show's consultants even included scientists from the world-famous RAND Corporation think tank.[2] Even today, the wide array of futuristic but realistic gadgets featured on the original *Star Trek* show is mesmerizing. *Star Trek* creations like the *U.S.S. Enterprise*'s transporter room ("Beam me up, Scotty!") and the crew's flip-open communicator devices still appear innovative even thirty years later.

Interestingly, every gadget in the *Star Trek* shows and movies has always had some real science behind it, a fact much appreciated by the Trekker community. The show's fans absolutely love that *Star Trek* has regularly challenged and shattered conventional wisdom through the years. "It's been an ongoing theme of *Star Trek* to try to be the first to do things that others haven't done," explains Dan Madsen, founder of the Official Star Trek Fan Club. "*Star Trek* has come up with a lot of unique concepts. These things all appeal to our sense of adventure and exploring what's really out there."[3]

Star Trek didn't stop daring to be different just by devising serious science fiction plots and gadgets, though. The original TV show also attacked the era's controversial social issues head on. Most notably, the first interracial kiss in TV history happened between Captain Kirk and Lieutenant Uhura on a *Star Trek* episode in 1968. Some mild controversy over "the kiss" ensued. Again, we're not suggesting that challenging conventional wisdom is ever easy. It definitely wasn't for *Star Trek,* and it likely won't be for your brand either. You need to be bold and brave. Cult brands offer the antithesis of conventional wisdom.

Always challenge what conventional wisdom says about your brand. Shatter it whenever possible. Be bold. Be brave. Be different. Conventional wisdom is just a crutch for conformity, while cult brands are shining symbols of nonconformity. Accept the unacceptable.

Conventional Wisdom Is Wrong Once Again

Oprah Winfrey is a perfect example of a successful cult brander who dared to be different and challenged conventional wisdom. After dominating the talk show genre for nearly a decade, Oprah abruptly announced in 1994 that she was going to abandon the realm of so-called "sensational TV."[4] Her show would no longer include tabloid topics and off-the-wall guests. Instead, she would offer only *solutions*—not *problems*. It was the kind of news that undoubtedly left Oprah's competitors snickering happily about her decision.

In truth, Oprah's ratings had slipped some by 1994 as her show suddenly began to look somewhat tame compared to her newer, more outlandish competition. Conventional wisdom at the time said that talk show viewers wanted to see more *not less* of the yelling and fighting that had suddenly turned the *Jerry Springer Show* and similar programs into home runs. This didn't matter to Oprah. Determined to turn her ratings around, she ignored the sneers of the skeptics and went ahead with the rollout of her new format based on self-improvement.

Clearly, the risks in making this move were huge. Yet like any good cult brand owner, Oprah knew that to stay on top she had to keep daring to be different. "Oprah made a very concious effort to differentiate her show and take the high road. At the time, she took quite a risk by doing this because there was no guarantee that audiences would watch something on a higher level," recalls *Chicago Sun-Times* TV and radio columnist Robert Feder, who has followed Oprah's talk show career since it began in Chicago in 1986.[5]

Oprah had decided that instead of trying to stoop lower and compete with the likes of Jerry Springer and Jenny Jones, she would head in the opposite direction and go higher. Her gut told her that her audiences wanted a show whose content was more fulfilling than the competition. And she was right. "Oprah took the tabloid talk show format and decided to dress up the neighborhood. She made her show the high-class version of this genre," says Dr. Robert Thompson, the Director of the Center for the Study of Popular Television at Syracuse University.[6]

Over seven years later, Oprah Winfrey is still the unequivocal Queen of Talk and owner of the highest-rated daytime talk show. Challenging conventional wisdom has worked marvelously well for her. Millions of TV viewers *did* in fact want a show with real substance, real topics, and real solutions. Oprah Winfrey proves that the makers of cult brands aren't afraid to take risks and stand by them. Strive for differentiation with your own brand each and every day. Be different. No idea is too radical for a cult brand company to consider unless everyone already likes it!

 Don't shackle your brand to conventional wisdom. With big risks come big rewards. Have you challenged the status quo lately? Or, do you brush aside radical ideas without a second thought? Have confidence in your instincts.

Ordinary People, Extraordinary Risks

WWE's Vince and Linda McMahon are both masters at challenging and shattering conventional wisdom. They've done it repeatedly now for over twenty years. In fact, one would be hard pressed to find a better example of big-time risk takers who started from such humble beginnings. They prove that *anyone* can build a cult brand. Neither Vince nor Linda McMahon grew up with a silver spoon in their mouth. In fact, Vince McMahon started out his career selling the *Encyclopedia Britannica* door-to-door, before eventually joining his father's small wrestling company in 1971.[7]

It was in 1982 when Vince and Linda first decided to really roll the dice in the wrestling world. And roll them they did. The two convinced Vince's father and his partners to sell them the family wrestling business. They agreed to make four quarterly payments of roughly $250,000 each. If Vince and Linda missed a payment, they would lose everything, and the business would revert back to the partners of Vince's father.[8] These were terms that would make even the most hardened banker blush, but the McMahons believed wholeheartedly in the potential of wrestling on a national scale, and they went ahead.

Their big gamble worked. Through relentless hustling, the McMahons were able to scrape together enough money to cover the four payments. Within a year, WWE was theirs. With the issue of ownership and control out of the way, the McMahons next set their eyes on another huge challenge—turning WWE into the first national wrestling brand. At the time, the idea of a national wrestling brand seemed highly unlikely, not to mention highly risky. Even in the early eighties, U.S. wrestling was still under the control of twenty or so regional promoters, who adhered to an unwritten rule that they wouldn't compete in each other's territories.

Building a national brand meant that the McMahons had to be willing to *break* this unwritten rule and compete directly with these established regional fiefdoms. Think hand-to-hand combat. Essentially, the McMahons had to be willing to go to war against every promoter in the country and each time risk losing their entire business. That's just what they did, and they did it quite creatively. While conventional wisdom said that the McMahons were crazy, they began by taking what little profits they had and paying local TV stations to regularly broadcast tapes of their company's wrestling matches.

No one in wrestling had ever considered this marketing idea before McMahon did, as he proudly recalled in a 1991 *Sports Illustrated* interview. "My major step was television on a local basis . . . The local guys were lazy. They weren't listening to the marketplace. We were so consumer oriented. We never lifted our ears from the ground. We gave the public what it wanted. We broke the mold."[9]

Not only did WWE break the hold of the regional wrestling companies with its barrage of local TV matches. The McMahons figured that wrestling fans nationwide who watched on television would eventually find themselves craving an exciting live WWE match in their own towns, instead of the tame offerings of the local promoter. They were right. WWE's risky TV broadcast strategy ended up working incredibly well.

Four years after the McMahons started their videotape blitzkrieg, only a handful of regional wrestling operators remained in business, and these survivors were running scared. WWE's promotions had not only won it thousands of new fans, it had also helped make the McMahons appear much larger and more powerful than they really were. "We did it with smoke and mirrors. If those promoters knew how little money I had, they could have killed me," recalled Vince McMahon in an interview with the *Hartford Courant*.[10]

Obviously, the promoters didn't kill Vince, Linda, or WWE. In fact, the McMahons took on new life. Their risk-taking redefined professional wrestling. Today, WWE is the only international brand of any consequence in professional wrestling,

---

RULE 2: Cult Brand Inventors Show Daring and Determination

Cult Brand Inc.	Others Inc.
Marketing Plan	**Marketing Plan**
■ Build and support genuine customer communities	■ Hire more telemarketers to call during dinner time
■ Listen to the feedback of followers and act on it	■ Send more annoying and irrelevant direct mail
■ Sponsor and support local groups and organizations	■ Distribute customer feedback boxes, but never open them
■ Try risky ideas if customers want it	■ Limit the length of customer service calls to save money

Cult branders give back and are willing to take significant risks! They spend their marketing dollars very differently than traditional companies. For example, Vans builds skate parks all across the United States to reward and connect with its customers, while its much larger competitors just blanket the airwaves and print media with flashy, pointless advertisements!

---

and it consistently produces many of the world's highest-rated cable TV shows and Pay-Per-View events. After starting basically from scratch, the McMahons now head an entertainment empire that generates over $400 million in sales annually.

A dozen other regional wrestling promoters could have been sitting where the McMahons are today, but they're not. Why? Because the McMahons were willing to dare to be different and embrace new ideas at every turn. They weren't willing to accept the notion that building a national wrestling brand was impossible. Ordinary people with the courage to take extraordinary risks build cult brands.

 The McMahons are ordinary people with the courage to take extraordinary risks. What's a marketing idea that your company considers extraordinarily risky? Is it risky because it's really a bad idea or risky only because it's never been tried before? Go do it.

Not Only Ordinary People, Ordinary Businesses

In a world increasingly filled with multinational conglomerates and sprawling financial empires, it's easy to believe that the "small guy" with his or her ordinary business just can't win anymore. The chieftains of Big Business would love to have us all believe that the small corner store is out of gas. And that the small businessperson is better off closing up shop while he or she still can run to the ranks of corporate America for safety. We're entering a future where only big companies can have big brands, so the conglomerates claim.

Don't believe any of this nonsense for a second. No matter what anyone tells you, any company—regardless of its size or industry—can still become a cult brand. Size, scale, and bulk don't build cult brands. What does is a combination of daring to be different and considerable risk-taking. Sure, multibillion-dollar companies will continue to be some of the biggest and most successful brand holders on the planet, but it's everyday ordinary people like you, the small business visionary, who run seemingly everyday ordinary stores and factories, that cultivate and create true cult brands.

How does this happen? Easy. Just look at *all* of the cult branders profiled in this book: the McMahons of WWE, Linus Torvalds of Linux fame, Steve Jobs of Apple, Oprah Winfrey, Jimmy Buffett, and *Star Trek* creator Gene Roddenberry. None of them has superhuman powers. These cult branders are all regular people who started with limited resources and dared to compete in industries that already had much larger, more established competitors. Most interesting, none of these individuals ran businesses that invented entire new industries from scratch.

For example, people were certainly wearing shoes for centuries before Vans Inc. was founded; yet this shoemaker is clearly a cult brand today. It's also true that Jimmy Buffett didn't create the concept of musical entertainment, and Gene Roddenberry didn't invent TV drama; yet both have spawned huge cult brands. And as much as Harley owners absolutely love their bikes, the truth is, motorcycles existed long before HD was ever founded. See how it works? Cult brands aren't built on the backs of radical new inventions or the creation of entire new industries; they are created by shattering conventional wisdom and constantly daring to be different in the way they *look, say,* and *feel.*

 Big brands aren't exclusively the domain of big companies. In fact, it's the small companies with limited resources, penchants for risk-taking, and "dare to be different" mentalities that more often than not spawn cult brands. Could this be a description of your business?

Have You Gone Out and "Bet the Company" Lately? • So, creating a cult brand has a lot to do with having the courage and determination to dare to be different, shatter conventional wisdom whenever possible, and take considerable risks. A good example of this kind of corporate derring-do is the management buyback and turnaround by Harley-Davidson in the early eighties. The thirteen Harley executives who bought back their company from manufacturing giant AMF in February of 1981 in an $80-million leveraged buyout pulled off the biggest example of a "bet the company" turnaround of a cult brand in recent memory.[11]

To say Harley had fallen on hard times by 1981 would be a drastic understatement. Not only were Japanese motorcycle makers bludgeoning the company on pricing, but the quality of the company's bikes had fallen to laughably low levels. In fact, a joke going around the company was that a Harley owner had to keep two HD bikes parked in the garage, one to ride and the other for spare parts. The joke had some truth to it. Harley was still building beautiful and powerful bikes, but they were for the most part unreliable and were no longer of HD's legendary quality.

It's easy to see why the conventional wisdom of the time held that Harley's then CEO Vaughn Beals and the other executives who cooperated in the buyback must have been a little bit crazy. These execs all risked their professional lives (jobs, salaries, reputation, you name it!) on a turnaround situation that at the time looked dire, even impossible. The funny thing is, the very fact that HD was in such poor health at the time is probably the main reason that the Beals-led turnaround proved successful. Quite simply, a whole company had its back against the wall and couldn't afford to fail! They *had* to make it. *Everything* was on the line.

In other words, Harley had no choice. The company had to drastically improve the quality of its motorcycles or watch itself go quickly out of business. It responded by copying Japanese techniques of production and quality control, as well as releasing in 1983 a new Harley engine dubbed the "Evolution," which helped put an end to oil leaks and related quality problems. Harley's management team also decided that if it ever hoped to regain market share it would have to start doing a better job of interacting and listening to its remaining customers. They began to focus on strengthening customer and dealer relationships, and this led to the eventual formation of the wildly successful Harley Owners Group, the HD-sponsored customer club, in 1983.[12]

The people behind cult brands are like great poker players. They often perform best in times of severe stress and uncertainty. In the case of Harley in its darkest hour in the 1980s, the entire organization from factory workers to management rallied together and battled the odds. Faced with possible extinction, HD never hesitated in making the needed "bet the company" decisions that would (and did) eventually differentiate its product from the competition. While companies with ordinary brands fold in these trying situations, companies with cult brands respond by daring to "let it all ride."

 Let it all ride. Throw all your chips onto the table and bet the company. Force your organization to periodically make "bet the company" decisions. Does this mean that the people behind cult brands are just crafty poker players in business suits? Compete with them and you'll find out!

The People Behind Cult Brands Never Quit

The people behind cult brands not only believe in taking significant risks, they never dream of quitting. Ever. Just look at legendary *Star Trek* creator Gene Roddenberry. Quitting was never ever in his vocabulary. Nor should it be for *any* aspiring cult brander reading this book. Take big risks and stick with them. In fact, if everyone thinks your new marketing or product idea makes a ton of sense, then the chances are you're doing something terribly wrong! The owners of brands that are safe tend to stay safe and undefined, while the owners of brands that take risks and stick with them demand customer attention and achieve eventual success.

For instance, Gene Roddenberry couldn't have been further away from fitting the mold of the typical Hollywood director. He wasn't born into a Hollywood family, and he didn't have any connections in the film industry. He was just an ordinary guy with a big dream to make it in Hollywood. A commercial airline pilot during the day, he enjoyed writing in his spare time and believed passionately in himself and his crazy ideas. In 1948, at the age of 26, Roddenberry decided to pursue his dream of writing full time and moved to Los Angeles. The first job he nabbed was in the public relations department of the Los Angeles Police Department.[13]

Building on his LAPD job, Roddenberry eventually worked his way into becoming a consultant to police TV shows of the time like *Dragnet*. This was a good start, but Roddenberry still hadn't yet hit the big time with his *own show*. In 1960, he began pitching the idea of *Star Trek* to the major Hollywood studios. As wacky as it sounds today, it took Roddenberry six years of hustling and pitching before NBC finally bit on *Star Trek*. Even then, Roddenberry's real challenges were only beginning. The original *Star Trek* pulled only mediocre ratings, and the series lasted only three short seasons before NBC cancelled it in 1969.

Anyone else but Roddenberry might have shelved his *Star Trek* ambitions right then and there and gone back to being a writer-cop. He didn't. Instead, Roddenberry hit the sci-fi lecture circuit hard, evangelizing to all who would listen about *Star Trek,* which by then was starting to run in TV syndication. At the same time, Roddenberry continued to constantly pitch the studios on doing a *Star Trek* motion picture. Amazingly, Roddenberry kept up this pace for an entire decade until 1979 when, after seeing the surprise success of a little movie called *Star Wars,* Paramount Studios finally gave him the green light to direct *Star Trek: The Motion Picture.*[14]

Not only was the first *Star Trek* film a big hit monetarily, grossing over $100 million, but it also validated Roddenberry's original vision, ensuring that *Star Trek* would be around for many years to come. When Roddenberry passed away at the age of seventy in 1991, he died knowing that his crazy idea had evolved into an important and lasting mainstay of American pop culture. Why did he succeed? Essentially, he dared to be different, took a series of big risks, and then didn't quit in the face of decades of adversity. When was the last time you shelved a new idea simply because a coworker criticized it? Quitters never have products that become cult brands.

 No one likes being called a quitter, yet most of us do it all too often. Quitting simply isn't in cult branders' DNA. They're fighters and survivors. Leaders not followers. When everyone else says they're likely going to fail, these fighters know they'll likely succeed.

The Beetle's Daring Battle
to Gain Acceptance in the U.S.A.

The story of the Volkswagen Beetle is another great example of the people behind a brand taking significant risks and shattering conventional wisdom against seemingly overwhelming odds. While today the Beetle is regarded as arguably the best selling car of all time, back in 1948 it was unknown in the U.S., and many sales types believed that Americans would *never* buy a VW. For one thing, the scars and memories of Germany during World War II were still very fresh. As far as many Americans were concerned in the late 1940s, Volkswagen and particularly the Beetle (Adolf Hitler had dubbed it "the people's car") were still symbols of Nazi Germany.

In reality, Dr. Ferdinand Porsche, founder of the legendary sports car company that still bears his name, designed the Volkswagen Beetle long before Hitler came to power in the 1930s. Still, the negative Nazi-Beetle connection continued in people's minds. This didn't deter Ben Pon, an enterprising exporter from Holland, who brought two Beetles into the U.S. in 1949. Unfortunately, Pon couldn't find *any* dealers or importers interested in buying his Beetles. In fact, the situation got so bad that "Pon soon had to sell his single sample car at a bargain price to pay his $800 hotel bill," as James Flammang noted in his book *Beetles, Buses & Beyond.*[15]

After Pon's failed effort, Volkswagen headquarters in Germany might safely have concluded that breaking into the U.S. market with the Beetle was out of the question. Not Volkswagen. Instead of following this conventional wisdom, shortly after the Pon fiasco VW brought twenty Beetles to the States, first to a private showing in New York City and then to the First U.S. International Trade Fair in Chicago, held in August of 1950. Although the Beetle's NYC and Chicago appearances didn't make it an overnight success in the U.S., the small, funny looking little car did get some U.S. press attention and real word-of-mouth buzz.

The rest as they say is history. VW's decision to hunker down, battle conventional wisdom, and focus on establishing itself in the U.S. market may go down as the savviest marketing decision in modern automotive history. In retrospect, Pon was simply ahead of the curve in his U.S. efforts, and many Americans in fact *didn't* have a problem owning "the people's car." In fact, they identified with its uniqueness. Given the opportunity to actually see and drive a Beetle, a significant chunk of the American public soon found themselves in love with the reliable and affordable little German car. Only a decade later in 1961, annual U.S. sales of the Beetle approached 200,000 units.

Probably most companies would have decided against entering the U.S. market if faced with the same negative signs as Volkswagen in 1949. No one likes to experience rejection and failure. It's never easy to build something incredibly different, take a big risk, watch it fall flat on its face, and still stick with it. Instead, that's when most of us want to pretend our outlandish marketing or product idea never happened. Volkswagen didn't do this. It stared failure in the face, kept its courage and determination intact, and believed that there was indeed a market for the Beetle in the U.S.A. Again, the people behind cult brands aren't quitters!

In 1949, VW didn't take the easy way out and accept defeat in the U.S. marketplace. It remained steadfast in its belief that Americans would eventually buy the Beetle. Hey, VW was right. When the people behind bland brands throw in the towel, the people behind cult brands just keep on fighting.

That Which Does Not Kill a Cult Brand Makes It Stronger

Outstanding cult brand companies like WWE, Star Trek, Oprah, and Volkswagen dared to be different, took considerable risks, and succeeded. Time and time again, these brands became leaders, not followers. This is not to say that cult branders are somehow always perfect and flawless. That's simply not the case. For all their courage, passion, and determination, cult branders still experience their share of outright failures. They are by no means infallible.

The people behind cult brands stumble, fall, and make mistakes just like people in any other business. In some cases, the mistakes they make are so severe that they even end up teetering on the edge of bankruptcy (as did Harley-Davidson) or actually end up in it (as did Vans). Yes, cult branders can "let it all ride" and still lose. Need some more examples of cult brands stumbling? How about Apple Computer? In 1993 it launched the Newton, the world's first handheld computer, only to pull the plug on its failed product in 1996. A few years later, the Palm Pilot came on the market and succeeded. Maybe Apple's timing was off.

Or what about WWE? Together with broadcasting partner NBC, it launched the XFL, an "extreme" professional football league, in 2000. Only a year later, the two companies had to abandon the venture after it drew dismal television ratings and shaky attendance at stadiums. WWE and NBC each lost reportedly $35 million on the experiment, and WWE's credibility took a temporary hit among Wall Street investors.[16] It's clear from talking to WWE CEO Linda McMahon, though, that she has no regrets about her brand's big XFL gamble. Says McMahon, "We've never been afraid to push the envelope in a way that makes sense."[17]

That's what's really amazing about cult brands' owners. They aren't afraid to fail, and when they do, instead of accepting defeat, they regroup and look to push the envelope again. Cult branders really take to heart the saying, "That which does not kill me makes me stronger." They're right, of course. The only way to truly experience tremendous success is to tempt defeat at every opportunity, which is exactly what cult brands do. Go for the extremes and move away from the bland-brand middle. Swing for the fences with your own brand. You too can survive failures. After all, no one ever talked about Babe Ruth's many strikeouts, but fans sure loved his hundreds of home runs!

That which does not kill a cult brand makes it stronger. Your brand will never have a chance to enjoy and maintain tremendous success until it has the opportunity to grapple with failure. Do you push your product or service to the edge? Be different. Aim for the extreme.

Cult Brands
Sell Lifestyles

Note to brand holders everywhere: Human beings want to have fun. Any time. Any place. Anywhere. Preferably, the more fun we can have, the better!

Fun on the weekends, fun at work, fun at home, fun on vacation, fun everywhere if humanly possible. So, come clean: Does your brand speak the language of this simple three-letter word? Is your brand f-u-n? Think about it. Does it put a smile on people's faces? Does it make people feel happy? Let's hope it does.

The human race's desire to have serious fun and happiness is certainly nothing new. We've been searching for ways to have fun for centuries now. In fact, the right to have fun is serious business. The Founding Fathers wrote into the Declaration of Independence that our inalienable human rights included not only Life and Liberty, but also the Pursuit of Happiness!

So, what exactly do fun and the pursuit of happiness have to do with cult branding? Absolutely everything. At their core, cult brands are *always fun*. They make us happy. They uplift our spirits. They cheer us up when we're down and give us confidence. They help us enjoy life. They not only make us feel better about ourselves, they also give us a temporary escape from the drudgery of everyday life.

Why do thousands of Parrot Heads flock to Jimmy Buffett concerts each year? To have fun. Why do thousands of Harley owners ride across the country to meet at weeklong motorcycle rallies in Sturgis and Daytona Beach each year? To have fun. Or why do thousands upon thousands of Apple faithful cram into MacWorld each year? Yep. To do some networking and business but basically to have fun.

Every cult brand in the world has a strong "fun factor" to it. Need more proof? Even a cult brand as seemingly technical and technology-oriented as the open-source operating system Linux was initially built for having fun. As Linux creator Linus Torvalds explained to a reporter from the *Washington Post* back in 1995, "Because we're not getting paid, the primary object is to have fun."[1]

The King of Fun Has a Secret

Out of the nine cult brands profiled in this book, entertainer Jimmy Buffett is unequivocally the King of Fun, and millions of fans who comprise the Parrot Head nation love him for it. The Buffett brand knows how to share fun with the world. Like or dislike Jimmy Buffett's Caribbean-flavored music, it's hard not to break into a big smile and have a heck of a good time at a Buffett concert. Where else in the world can you see thousands of happy people celebrating in a parking lot dressed in Hawaiian shirts, grass skirts or shark-fin hats, and drinking frozen margaritas and eating cheeseburgers?

"It's extreme escapism! Jimmy is a master of painting such a vivid picture of life in the palm trees drinking margaritas and just having a great time," says Scott Nickerson, a long-time Parrot Head and also one half of A1A, the most well-known Jimmy Buffett tribute band. "Jimmy paints great pictures with his songs. You can feel yourself there."[2]

Where exactly is *there?* For a Buffett fan, "there" likely is a tropical beach where the sun always shines, the water is always warm and crystal clear, bills never have to be paid, good friends are always around, and the frozen margaritas and frosty Coronas never stop coming.

Now we ask you. Who wouldn't like to be part of this care-free fantasy world even for just a little while? Most people surely wouldn't complain. Some surf, sand, and fun sure works! Is it really any surprise that Jimmy Buffett has been able to build such an incredibly loyal legion of fans over the years? While most music artists focus their attention on making and selling albums and videos, Buffett aims at selling his fans the opportunity for temporary escapism through his music, books, concerts, and Margaritaville restaurants.

Like every good cult brander, Buffett doesn't focus his efforts on simply selling a product or service; he sells a lifestyle. Buffett's music essentially offers an ongoing state of mind and set of ideals that his loyal followers can carry around through life. This lifestyle is what Parrot Heads around the world are really buying. They are purchasing the opportunity to fulfill their passions and dreams with like-minded individuals through various activities, be it a road trip to a Buffett concert, meeting with local Parrot Heads for drinks at happy hour, or volunteering with other Parrot Heads to help a nonprofit organization.

Many of Buffett's fans fully understand that by buying Buffett's products they are also buying a unique lifestyle. "I like the laid-back lifestyle that Jimmy conveys. Everyone likes to envision themselves on a sunny beach, drinking a cold beer and relaxing," says Billy Peoples, cofounder and manager of the Parrot Head Web ring and a loyal Parrot Head for the past twenty-five years.[3]

Clearly, selling a lifestyle works. It's worked marvelously for Buffett for decades now, and there's no reason it won't work for your brand as well. Provide your customers with an escape. Help them have fun. We all love brands that aid us in the pursuit of happiness.

 The pursuit of happiness. Human beings all chase after it, and so do your potential customers. People want products and services that make them feel good. So, is your brand fun? Does it put a smile on people's faces? Does it even make you happy? Only you know the answers.

Understanding Self-Fulfillment

Temporary escapism is only one slice of what the people behind cult brands serve up to their customers. Always keep in mind that there are numerous other places and brands where people can go to have fun and escape for a while. A hearty dose of fun alone doesn't ensure that a brand will attract and retain a loyal following. The people behind cult brands also understand people's need for self-fulfillment or the self-actualization that behavioral expert Abraham Maslow describes.

RULE 3: Cult Brands Sell Lifestyles

Questions that every aspiring cult brander should ask themselves:

- Does your product or service make your customers feel good?
- Does your product or service put a smile on people's faces?
- At their core, cult brands are *always* fun. Is your brand F-U-N?
- Does your brand provide temporary escapism for its followers?
- What passions and dreams does your brand help fulfill?
- Does your brand promote self-empowerment and self-fulfillment?
- Cult brands champion the freedom of the individual. Does yours?
- Is your brand pervasive (high-frequency) in the lives of its customers?

Cult Brands are masters of selling lifestyles—not just products and services—to their legions of customers. By selling lifestyles, Cult Brands are able to bundle feelings of temporary escapism, self-fulfillment, and self-empowerment all into experiential "product packages" for sale. Remember: People all have dreams, fantasies, passions, and aspirations. Cult Brand companies help fulfill them.

We probably all were told as children and again as adults that if you can *find something you really love to do and then do it, you'll never work a day in your life.* After all, wouldn't it be great if your job didn't really *seem* like a job at all but felt more like a hobby? Sort of a never-ending nine-to-six vacation. What if every day of work was really fun, and most important, fulfilling? What if you looked forward to going to work every Monday morning? Don't laugh. Some lucky souls are actually able to turn their passions and dreams into paying jobs. But they're a rare bunch.

For the vast majority of us, it's incredibly difficult to follow down this path. Unfortunately, while following our passions may be incredibly fulfilling, it doesn't pay the bills. If we want to eat, we need a regular income.

Still, somewhere deep in the back of our minds, humans yearn for more out of life than a regular paycheck or material items like fancy new cars or nice big houses. Try as we might, most of us simply can't escape feeling the need to pursue and try to fulfill our true dreams and passions. In fact, one needs to look no further than the explosion in the popularity of the Linux operating system over the past decade to see that even the most successful of us never stop seeking greater self-fulfillment.

Otherwise, how can one explain why many of the world's best software developers, individuals who easily make six-figure salaries at megacorporations during the day, volunteer their time and program for free on open-source projects like Linux at night? Simple. Programmers obviously receive a much deeper feeling of gratification and fulfillment from working on Linux than they get at their corporate day jobs. Since Linux is "open source," developers are free to write and share code as they please with their peers, instead of being commanded by a boss to write code that may hold little interest for them.

"When you're a programmer, a lot of times you go home and write code because it's fun and a hobby. It's something that you're interested in doing. You get a deeper satisfaction that you don't necessarily get out of your job," says Slashdot.org founder Rob Malda. "Everyone has an inherent desire to create that comes from within, not from your boss."[4]

The bossless Malda should know. He started Slashdot as a simple hobby Web site in September 1997 because he enjoyed graphic design and the sharing of his graphical creations and thoughts on tech topics with others. Today, with hundreds of thousands of monthly visitors, Slashdot is probably the world's largest online community for the discussion of Linux and "news for nerds," as Slashdot's tag line proudly says.

Linux is not unique in serving as an outlet for a group of individuals (in this case, programmers) to pursue their dreams and passions. *All* cult brands, from Linux and Apple to Jimmy Buffett and Oprah Winfrey, on some level serve as tools of self-actualization for their customers. These cult branders don't just sell products or services in the traditional sense. In essence, they give their customers the opportunity to *enjoy a temporary escape into a sanctuary of self-fulfillment.* For some, this escape may mean partying at an all-day Jimmy Buffett concert, while for others it may mean riding a Harley-Davidson motorcycle. The makers of successful cult brands sell passions and dreams that devoted customers associate with their products and services.

 Passions and dreams. We all have them. What are the passions and dreams of your customers? How can your product or service provide your customers with a temporary escape? Cult brands help provide their followers with sanctuaries of self-fulfillment.

Cult Brands Intertwine Themselves Around Passions and Dreams

Passions and dreams. We all have them. These are the things we look forward to when we're snowed under with paperwork at the office, shuttling the kids off to soccer practice, or stuck in bumper-to-bumper traffic. These are the activities and hobbies that provide us with a much needed release and a temporary escape from the responsibilities and realities of everyday life. While these activities are different for each of us, they are still remarkably all alike, since they accomplish the same goals of self-fulfillment and temporary escapism.

The makers of cult brands tap directly into the power of customers' passions and dreams by intertwining their products and services directly around these activities. Look at Vans shoes and its tight relationship with extreme sports like skateboarding. It's no accident that Vans sponsors and organizes dozens of extreme sports events each year. It knows that this is the best way to connect with its customers. For many teenagers and young adults, an activity like skateboarding *is* their passion. In the words of skateboarding legend Stacy Peralta, skateboarding provides kids with a "viable myth."[5]

After all, what is more liberating for a teenager than hopping onto a skateboard and riding for a few minutes each day without having to worry about chores, homework, or even parental control for a little while? For a teenager, a skateboard is temporary escapism and self-fulfillment on four wheels and some wood. No doubt about it, it is a perfect activity for a cult brand to become intertwined with. With this in mind, Vans has gone out of its way the past seven years to sponsor and promote activities like music concerts and sporting events that appeal to the extreme sports and skateboarding set.

As Vans CEO Gary Schoenfeld told *Business Week* magazine in an interview last year, "Our vision is not to hit our target audience over the heads with ads but to integrate ourselves into the places where they are most likely to be."[6] Schoenfeld also shared his views on lifestyle with *Inc.* magazine back in 1999, telling the publication, "Kids don't relate to direct hard-sell advertising. They see through a company that's just spending a lot of money to attract their attention. Our strategy is to ingratiate ourselves more into their lifestyle."[7]

In addition to developing high-profile events for its customers like the Vans Triple Crown and the Vans Warped Tour,

Vans has also in recent years begun building and operating its own skateboard parks. Vans now operates a dozen such parks around the country, each filled with thousands of square feet of rideable space for both skateboarders and BMX bikers of all skill levels. Of course, each Vans-branded park also includes a retail shop with Vans shoes and merchandise. These parks give the people at Vans a unique way to weave their products into the regular activities of their customers.

 Cult brands understand the power of selling lifestyles. Vans connects with its customers by sponsoring music festivals and extreme sports events, as well as operating its own skateboard parks. What kinds of activities are popular with your customers?

Cult Brands Combine Self-Empowerment with Passions and Dreams

The most important extension of self-fulfillment and self-actualization that many cult brand companies provide for their customers is self-empowerment. While the exact definition of self-empowerment for each person may be different, at its core the meaning is essentially the same for all of us. Being self-empowered means being in control of one's own destiny. Self-empowerment represents power and freedom of the individual rather than power and control by a system, be it the government or a group. No one likes to feel like a miniscule pawn on a giant chessboard.

We've all felt the need to rebel at one time or another, whether that meant participating in a political march or refusing to pay a speeding ticket we felt we didn't deserve. Without a doubt, while we humans inherently feel a need to form groups with leaders and rules, we also cherish our freedom to make decisions and choices as individuals. We all want self-empowerment. However, to truly reach a feeling of self-fulfillment at any task or activity one must first believe that he or she can actually control his or her own destiny and decisions. We want the individual not the system to be in control.

Apple Computer is the epitome of self-empowerment and self-fulfillment combined in one brand. How else to describe a cult brand whose original slogan for the Macintosh was "the computer for the rest of us?" Of course, "the rest of us" were those brave individuals who wanted to control their own destinies and break free of *the system's* controlling grip and authoritarian ways. In the eighties, Apple painted this dark controlling force as being IBM, while in the nineties it became Microsoft and Bill Gates. Despite the change in villains, the underlying story remains unchanged. Apple consistently markets its products as tools for self-empowerment in the customer's ongoing personal war against society's control freaks.

"Apple absolutely associated itself with liberation pop culture. Its themes were rebellion against authority and rebellion against conformity. There was a real focus on self-realization and self-empowerment," recalls Christopher Escher, a former Vice President of Corporation Communications for Apple. While Escher left Apple in 1996 after spending more than a decade at the company, he still marvels at how much Apple's marketing message accomplished. "They turned computers, which are essentially a product for business people to crunch numbers with, into symbols of self-realization and liberation against social constraints."[8]

Apple is not alone among cult brands that again and again hit on this self-empowerment theme. Linux is another. As Linux advocate Eric Raymond stated to the *Washington Post* in 1998, "Open source is a way to give power to individuals and deny coercive power to the government and monopolistic corporations."[9]

Or what about Oprah Winfrey? Her brand is clearly a tool for self-empowerment. Her millions of TV viewers undoubtedly feel more in control of their lives after watching one of her uplifting shows, reading *O,* her monthly magazine, or picking up one of Oprah's Book Club selections, which often contain self-empowerment themes. Through her strong self-empowerment messages, Winfrey long ago transcended the realm of her talk show competitors. "Oprah became much more than just a talk show host. She became a lifestyle," says Dr. Robert Thompson, the expert on the study of popular television.[10]

And take a look at the Star Trek brand. Each *Star Trek* show, movie, and book speaks of a bright future where the human race doesn't blow itself up, and man is able to achieve incredible feats on his own and with other species. *Star Trek* helps prove that human beings as a race aren't helpless or hopeless. Earth endures. Jeff Greenwald, travel writer and author of *Future Perfect: How Star Trek Conquered Planet Earth,* goes as far as to say, "For some fans, Star Trek is the thing that really gives their life meaning."[11]

 Self-fulfillment and self-empowerment go hand in hand. The two need each other, and your brand needs both. How does your product or service help empower your customers? How does it celebrate the individual? Cult brand companies champion the freedom of the individual.

Self-Empowerment: A Foundation for Selling Lifestyles • How can a brand holder go about weaving this self-empowerment theme into his or her own business? Remember the three amigos of *look, say,* and *feel* from Rule 1? Not only can look, say, and feel differentiate your brand in the marketplace, but this trio also offers a direct path for building your brand's self-empowerment message.

Let's start with *look.* Do your product's design and features give power and control back to the individual? Do its design and features convey a sense of rebellion against conformity? Some products naturally work better than others at visually conveying self-empowerment. Motorcycles, for example, are traditionally thought of as symbols of freedom and nonconformity (do Hell's Angels ring a bell?). However, Harley-Davidson goes beyond this basic assumption and cranks it up a notch with its loud growling engines, bold signature body styling, and ostentatious amounts of chrome on its bikes.

So, what can you do if your product or service's design or features don't *look* particularly empowering? Focus your attention instead on optimizing your brand's marketing message and what it actually *says* to your customers and helps make them *feel* as individuals. This is where Oprah Winfrey excels. Day after day, Oprah shares with her audience a message of hope, happiness, and love for self and others. Her self-improvement topics are particularly empowering for her followers, because they cover issues that are within the viewer's control to change and improve. The *Oprah Winfrey Show* is a daily celebration of freedom for the individual.

Yet the successes of Harley-Davidson and Oprah Winfrey go far beyond creating brands that demonstrate strong self-empowerment feelings through *look, say,* and *feel.* While this is a great start, feelings of self-empowerment alone are typically not enough to hook a customer for the long haul. Your loyal customers feel self-empowered by using your particular brand's product or service, but they also must derive a great sense of self-fulfillment from interacting with the brand. In other words, using cult brands gives customers a feeling of control of their own destinies and also makes them feel they are *being all that they can be*. They are temporarily fulfilling a dream or passion.

That's why cult brands essentially sell lifestyles, not just their actual products or services. Selling *lifestyles* offers cult branders the opportunity to bundle feelings of temporary escapism, self-fulfillment, and self-empowerment all together nicely into experiential "product packages" for sale. Sell lifestyles—not products. Remember, Vans isn't marketing shoes or shirts. It's selling customers the opportunity to become part of the Vans lifestyle—enjoying extreme sports events, all-day music festivals, and skateboard parks all amongst like-minded individuals, while of course *wearing* Vans shoes, T-shirts, and gear.

Look at the Harley lifestyle. HD doesn't just sell a potential customer a motorcycle and HD-branded accessories or merchandise to wear. The Harley-Davidson company sells its customers the opportunity to join local Harley Owners Groups, attend bike rallies around the country, and go on weekend rides in their area with fellow bikers. Much like the Vans customer, a Harley customer essentially buys into the opportunity to take part in activities that help temporarily fulfill his or her real passions and dreams. The HD motorcycle is just a tool, almost a membership card, into the customer's self-actualization process.

Star Trek, too, sells its own lifestyle. Whether Paramount realizes it entirely or not, it's *not* selling *Star Trek* movies and shows. Its customers are buying into the opportunity to join the Star Trek lifestyle and become involved with a local Star Trek fan club and attend any of the hundreds of weekend Star Trek conventions held each year. Star Trek gives people passionate about space exploration and quality science fiction the opportunity to interact. As *Star Trek Communicator* magazine publisher Dan Madsen explains, "Star Trek has helped its fans achieve their dreams and fantasies." Doesn't this sound like self-actualization, self-empowerment, and escapism to you?

 By selling lifestyles, not just products or services, the makers of cult brands provide their customers with the opportunity to pursue dreams. What are you selling your customers? The key to an exciting new lifestyle or just a useful product or service?

Enhance Customers' "Touch Points" with Your Brand

In the mid-nineties, things were looking pretty grim for Apple Computer. The company was steadily losing money, it lacked strong leadership at the top, and the firm's overall share of the PC market was continuing to slip. In a nutshell, things were not well in the Mac nation. While Apple continued to have millions of loyal customers around the world, it endured this period thinking that any day a larger competitor would buy it. Or the corporation might fail outright. Of course, neither of these things happened.

Then, after more than a decade away from Apple, company cofounder Steve Jobs came back aboard the Mac mother ship (in a surprise move) as interim CEO in 1997. As most readers will remember, Jobs, through a savvy combination of internal cost-cutting, revamped marketing, and new product launches (driven by the wildly popular iMac), turned Apple around. Today, Apple is again profitable, cash-rich, re-energized, and maintaining its estimated 5 percent world share of the PC market.[12]

So, where does Apple go next? How does it grow? This is a question that decision makers at all cult brands eventually face at one time or another. In the case of the folks at Apple, they are now focusing all of their efforts on strengthening and enhancing the "Mac lifestyle" by working to increase the frequency that their customers interact with the Apple brand on a daily basis. To really sell a 24/7 lifestyle brand means being pervasive. With this in mind, Apple is now pushing to turn the Mac into what it calls the "hub of a digital lifestyle," basically a home base for managing a Mac user's everyday music, photo, and video devices.[13]

To help accelerate this process, in 2001 Apple announced the launch of the sleekly designed iPod, its own portable music player. You guessed it. The device *only* works with a Mac computer. Other portable digital devices from Apple are likely in the works. In another move to help strengthen the Mac lifestyle, Apple is also launching its own retail Apple Stores in high-traffic malls around the country. Half of each Apple Store is dedicated to showing customers what activities *they can achieve* with a Mac's help like recording and editing their own movies and their own music.[14] It looks like self-empowerment and self-fulfillment are at the top of the list for in-store marketing by Apple!

It's too early to speculate whether Apple's launch of the iPod and its new Apple Stores will work or not. Nevertheless, Apple is going in the direction every aspiring cult brander should be moving. How can you create more frequency and interaction for your brand with potential customers? What are other activities that comprise the lifestyle you're trying to sell? Intertwine your brand with these activities. Selling a lifestyle means having a frequent and continuous relationship with your customers. The more "touch points" you can develop between your customer and brand, the better.

 So, you want your product or service to become and stay a cult brand. That means you're looking to sell a lifestyle not just a product. This means that your brand must become pervasive in the lives of your customers. How can you build additional customer "touch points" for your brand? Think frequency.

Cult Brands Build "Living Monuments"

All of the nine cult brands profiled in this book have people behind them who have dealt with the issue of maintaining sales growth, as well as sustaining strong customer loyalty. These successful people have built frequency by creating more and more customer touch points for their brands. Apple Computer isn't the only company betting that the best way to grow its customer base is by building more "living monuments" (in its case, Apple Stores) that celebrate their brand's lifestyle. Don't forget the old adage, *out of sight, out of mind.* Customers need many *visual* and *tangible* "touch points" to help remind them of the passions and dreams your brand can fulfill.

WWE has two new living monuments geared to customer recruitment and retention. In the year 2000 the McMahons opened

WWE New York, a WWE-themed restaurant in Times Square. And over the past two years they produced with cable channel MTV a popular weekly behind-the-scenes series, *Tough Enough*, that follows aspiring WWE wrestlers. Both WWE New York and the *Tough Enough* series give the McMahons excellent opportunities to showcase the WWE lifestyle to potential new fans, while building additional brand frequency with existing WWE followers.

Harley-Davidson has also entered the themed restaurant business, having opened in recent years large Harley-Davidson Cafés in both New York and Las Vegas, two of the world's largest tourist destinations. Both heavily trafficked cafés are chock full of Harley bikes, information, and merchandise. Over the past decade, HD has also invested significant time and money in remodeling many of its dealerships (think dozens of *mini-monuments*). These designer stores, each filled with Harley bikes, merchandise, and a lounge, are geared to feel warm and inviting to potential new customers.

Even Paramount has realized the importance of building a *living monument* to bring new customers into the Star Trek fold. In January 1998, Paramount, in partnership with Hilton Hotels, opened a $70-million attraction in Las Vegas called Star Trek: The Experience. The attraction includes a realistic Star Trek adventure aboard the *U.S.S. Enterprise* complete with a four-minute simulation ride, a museum on space history, and a recreation of a 24th century Star Trek restaurant and bar.[15] Star Trek: The Experience's high touch, high-sensory environment is lifestyle marketing at its best.

Volkswagen has also thrust itself into the *living monument* act in a unique way, with the opening last year of Autostadt, a self-styled car theme park in Germany. The park expects to attract a whopping one million tourists per year. Autostadt, literally translated as Auto City, is a 62-acre entertainment park and automotive museum highlighting the rich history and mystique of Volkswagen cars like the Beetle. As *Salon.com* noted, the opening of the park is "an attempt to make buying their product not just a purchase, but a pageant."[16] Without a doubt, Autostadt represents an innovative introduction to the Volkswagen lifestyle.

The small businessperson reading this section should absolutely try to understand that *any* brand of *any* size can build its own living monument today. A company doesn't need to spend millions of dollars for its brand to be successful. Size doesn't necessarily equal success. Starting small is fine. There are many ways to build frequency with your customers and leverage this living monument concept. A small retailer who does something as simple as hire an interior decorator to remodel the store to make it look more inviting is off to a good start. Or, if you're the owner of a small service-provider business, you might tell your salespeople to make more frequent calls and visits to clients, even when they *don't* have any new services to sell.

 WWE New York and MTV's *Tough Enough.* AutoStadt. Star Trek: The Experience. Harley-Davidson Cafés. Cult brands build *living monuments* that help celebrate the lifestyles they are selling. How can your brand create touch points and build greater frequency with your customers?

Rule 4

Listen to the Choir

and Create

Cult Brand Evangelists!

THE WORLD almost never really got to know Captain Kirk, Mr. Spock, Dr. "Bones" McCoy, and the rest of the illustrious crew of the *U.S.S. Enterprise.* One of the world's greatest cult brands was almost dead upon arrival.

As hard as it is to believe today after all its success, the original *Star Trek* television series almost didn't make it to a third season. While the show drew respectable ratings its first year, the ratings went down during the second season, and the show was hardly considered a hit by network executives at NBC. Then, in December of 1967, when the cancellation of Gene Roddenberry's intergalactic baby looked highly likely, the very "unlikely" happened.

Word quickly spread among science-fiction fans that *Star Trek* was being cancelled. That's when the husband and wife team of Bjo and John Trimble entered the picture. The two sci-fi buffs quickly reacted to the news by developing a "Save *Star*

Trek" letter-writing campaign. Gene Roddenberry got down in the trenches with the Trimbles and helped drum up support. The results of their tireless efforts were that NBC received a barrage of letters from fans begging the network to bring the show back. NBC agreed, and Trekkers got to see a third season of their beloved series.[1]

In *Star Trek's* history, the Trimbles' letter-writing campaign stands out as a monumental moment for both Trekkers and Paramount. Although NBC again cancelled the series after the one-year reprieve, *Star Trek* by then consisted of 79 episodes, enough shows to warrant Paramount selling the reruns to the syndication market. Without a third season, syndication would have been a long shot for Paramount and Roddenberry. Instead, *Star Trek* snuck into syndication and since then has evolved into the most popular syndicated show in television history.

Today, *Star Trek* is known fondly as "The Franchise" among Paramount executives. It is a cash cow like no other. The studio has grossed hundreds of millions from *Star Trek* sales over the past thirty years. Nine motion pictures. Five television series. Dozens of best-selling books and an endless amount of licensed Star Trek merchandise. None of this would ever have come to fruition if it had not been for Roddenberry pleading for support from his fans, and the Trek nation's

---

 Preach and listen to the choir. That's how brand evangelists are made. Do you really listen to what your customers want? Or do you spend all day giving them lip service? If you want your marketing message to be heard, you have to be willing to listen!

---

wholehearted response. Paramount and NBC then showed enough sense to understand the passionate fan reaction and bring *Star Trek* back for its third season.

Stop Marketing to the "Pagans" and Preach to the Choir

The gut instinct of most companies, large and small, is to try and build their own cadre of brand evangelists by spending countless sums of money on mass marketing. As if by sheer force and repetition, these executives think a brand can turn a handful of disinterested consumers into a fervent pack of John the Baptists overnight. You know the classic drill. Run lots of glossy print ads. Run tons of network and cable television spots. Beat your potential customers into submission. Although this list of tactics might sound good, the thinking behind this approach is flawed.

Using mass marketing to convert "pagans" is rarely where your company will find and develop its true brand evangelists. The trick is, you have to preach to the choir. That's right. Focus your efforts on satisfying the happy customers in the "congregation" you *already* have! These are the customers who *already* listen to your marketing messages, *already* know your product, *already* know your brand, and *already* feel real excitement for your company's product. Preach to them. Make them feel loved and accepted. Shoemaker Vans Inc. took this approach over twenty-five years ago and is now reaping the rewards.

While Vans is today known as a symbol of alternative sports like skateboarding and snowboarding, the company didn't start out this way. The original dream of Paul Van Doren and his family was simply to manufacture shoes and sell them directly to the public, which he did when Vans opened its first small shop in 1966. Then in the mid-seventies Southern California skateboarders started wearing Vans shoes. Unlike any other shoe manufacturer at the time, Vans accepted these customers and actually began catering to the desires and needs of the, then, renegade skateboarding crowd.

In fact, Vans was the first shoe company to start paying well-known skateboarders to wear its shoes. "They were the only company at that time that would pay us, the skateboarders, any money whatsoever," recalls pro skateboarding legend Stacy Peralta. "Not only did other companies not want to sponsor us, but it's as if they didn't even want us riding their products!"[2]

Essentially, Vans took skateboarders—consumers that in the seventies were treated like lepers by the rest of corporate America—and celebrated them as champions. Vans preached to the choir and then listened to their response. One thing skateboarders were clamoring for at that time was multi-colored shoes. Vans listened and soon came up with a red and blue shoe designed by Peralta and another pro skateboarder, Tony Alva. When the new shoe thrilled skaters, Vans was well on its way to having its own pack of true brand evangelists. Preach. Listen. That's the real ticket for cult branders!

 Break away from the notion of mass marketing as a conversion tool for building evangelists. Look at the congregation of customers you already have. Preach to them. Listen to their response. Your best potential brand evangelists are already sitting in the pews!

RULE 4: Listen to the Choir and Create Cult Brand Evangelists!

The Blueprint for Creating a Brand Evangelist

- Search amongst your existing customer base and identify the true members of your *choir*.

- Now reach out to your choir and help bring them together as a unified "brand congregation."

- Ask them for their honest feedback (praise, comments, and criticisms). Then, listen intently!

- Find out what your brand *really means* to your choir. Why do they *love* your brand?

- Remember: Listen to the choir's wants and needs—not the suggestions of "potential" or possible customers.

- Take heed of the choir's best suggestions and turn them into reality. Cater to your choir's wishes.

- Show your choir that you *really care* and they can't help but become brand evangelists for you!

Cult Branders are committed to serving the wants and needs of their existing customers. There is no shame in "preaching to the choir." In fact, it's one of the smartest things you can do with your brand. Listen and react to the wants and needs of the followers that are *already attracted* to your brand. Never abandon your choir. Without a choir, your brand has no evangelists!

Margaritaville's Big Surprise

Preaching and listening to the choir doesn't have to cost a small fortune. Think TLC. As long as a company shows Tender Loving Care in its treatment of customers, they will respond accordingly. Jimmy Buffett is a master at finding cost-effective and unique ways to reward his most dyed-in-the-wool brand evangelists, the Parrot Heads. While it would be easy after touring for three decades playing virtually the same songs night after night to be less than friendly and grateful at times, Buffett is always good to his fans.

"I've never heard him say anything disparaging about his fans," says Billy Peoples, a long time Buffett fan and cofounder of the popular Parrot Head Web ring. "Jimmy always gets up for each performance and thanks us for coming and supporting him. He always does that," explains Peoples admiringly.[3]

In addition to thanking his fans after each show, Buffett also takes time out to express his support and gratitude to the Parrot Heads in Paradise organization. Each year, PHIP holds an annual convention in Key West (of course!) affectionately called "Meeting of the Minds." And every year Jimmy Buffett creates and sends a playful videotaped welcome that thousands of Parrot Heads see at the opening of the convention.

The big screen video greeting is a unique opportunity for Buffett to reward his most devoted fans and tell them that he is thinking of them. "Every year, he'll be silly and say something in the video welcome like 'Have fun and don't steal too many of my Margaritaville glasses!'" jokes Parrot Heads in Paradise founder Scott Nickerson.[4]

At the seventh annual Meeting of the Minds in 1998, Jimmy Buffett took the idea of preaching to the choir to the next level. While members of Buffett's band, the Coral Reefers, had always attended and played at the convention, Buffett himself had never made an appearance. That's why Parrot Heads were pleasantly shocked when Buffett appeared out of nowhere in Key West that year and started jamming with all of his fans the Saturday night of the convention. Spending only a few hours of his time, Buffett created good will with thousands of his best customers that will probably last forever!

In addition to his video welcomes and surprise appearance at that annual convention, Jimmy Buffett has also come up with another nice way to reward his brand evangelists. For years now, Buffett's management company has reserved a handful of group tickets for local Parrot Head clubs when a Buffett concert is happening in their area. While this ticket program takes little more than time and effort for Buffett's team, it goes a long way towards further cementing the strong bond between Buffett and his core fans.

 If Jimmy Buffett, one of the biggest grossing artists ever, can still show incredible gratitude to his fans millions of dollars later, why can't you do it also? You can! Your brand is waiting and ready. How can you remind your best customers that you're always thinking of them?

Becoming the "Apple" of Their Customer's Eye

Remember the old golden rule, *Do unto others as you would have them do unto you,* that we all learned back in grade school? Of course you do. Well, following the golden rule may be the key to building profitable customer relationships and nurturing brand evangelists. Another way to interpret the rule is, you can't expect your customers to develop into loyal followers and listen to your marketing messages if your company habitually ignores what they have to say! While every business likes to give lip service to serving the needs of its customers, the reality is that most companies are lousy listeners. When customers figure this out, they penalize those brands.

Apple Computer has a variety of interesting ways of preaching and listening to the choir. For starters, Apple hosts a User Group University twice a year at Macworld New York and San Francisco. At each User Group University, roughly one hundred Mac

User Group leaders from around the world meet with each other for a full day of workshops and conversations about Apple's latest products. Apple showers all attendees with free logo merchandise, as well as employee discounts at the company store. Not only does Apple come away with invaluable feedback from a great group of customers, but it re-energizes the Mac's key faithful.[5]

In addition to its User Group Universities, Apple has also put into place what it calls Apple Regional Liaisons and the Apple User Group Advisory Board. Apple asks individuals who run successful Mac User Groups in their communities to participate and to help Apple work with less successful user groups in the region. Basically, these regional liasons and the advisory board serve as Apple's eyes and ears on the street. They continually gather feedback for Apple and look for Mac success stories to share. The advisory board meets twice a year at Macworld, monthly by conference call, and continually via e-mail, leaving little doubt that Apple *cares* for its brand evangelists!

By following this game plan, Apple is able to give its customers the product enhancements they really want instead of guessing what the whims of their customers might be. "Revise your product or service for the people who are *already adopting it*," says former Apple Fellow and bestselling business book author Guy Kawasaki, "not for the people who say, for example, 'If only you had a letter quality print driver, I would buy a Macintosh.'"[6] In other words, the marketers at cult brands always remember that a bird in the hand is worth two in the bush.

Brand evangelists love attention and feed off it. Plain and simple. The front office at every cult brand understands this. After all, when was the last time you *didn't* like the special treatment of getting the best seats in a restaurant or a chance to jump ahead in a long line somewhere? Probably never! Budding brand evangelists are just like the rest of us. They're ordinary people with wants and needs. Show them you appreciate their support, that you care for their input and actually *implement their suggestions,* and you're one step closer to having a lasting customer and an invaluable new brand ally.

 Follow Apple's lead. Does your company have a customer advisory board in place? Have you ever hosted events and workshops where your customers can openly share their real feelings about your brand? The feedback you get when you tap the pulse of your brand evangelists is invaluable.

Use Your Evangelists to Repair Those Lukewarm Relationships

Star Trek isn't the only cult brand that arose from a feverish letter-writing campaign from its fans. Unbeknownst to many, the New Beetle when it was first unveiled in 1994 at the North American International Auto Show was only a concept car. Volkswagen executives at the time viewed their new model as little more than a cool design concept and had no immediate plans to put their "nostalgia car" into production. To their surprise, by 1996 Volkswagen had received over 35,000 letters and phone calls from people of all ages and backgrounds begging them to make the New Beetle a reality, which they of course did in early 1998.[7] Customers basically willed the New Beetle into being!

While the Volkswagen company today is not very involved with independent VW clubs, a number of Volkswagen dealers still help support them. It's a tradition that's continued for over thirty years in some places. Rich Kimball, organizer of the VW Classic, the largest annual VW car show in the U.S., remembers his local Volkswagen dealer sponsoring the Newport Beach Volkswagen Club in California when he joined it in 1966. "One week out of the month we had our meetings at the dealership," says Kimball. "They opened up the service department and let us put our cars up on the lifts. They even had a few mechanics there to help us change our oil."[8]

Realizing that it had done only a so-so job in recent years of communicating with the vintage VW community, Volkswagen of America in 1996 hosted the "Generations of Innovation Summit" at its headquarters in Auburn Hills, Michigan. The summit brought together key players in the vintage community, and for two days, show organizers, journalists, and club promoters interacted with VW's top brass. Not only that, they also drove all of VW's new cars, toured its North American headquarters, had dinner with VW's executives, and shared their thoughts on the forthcoming New Beetle.[9]

The net result of the summit was to show the vintage VW community, the people who are the heart and soul of Beetle mania, that their opinions still mattered. Volkswagen went back to its roots of preaching to the choir and then listening. It visibly cared again. The vintage VW community was noticeably tickled that Volkswagen had offered the olive branch. "They picked our brains about what we thought about the cars," says the VW Classic's Kimball who clearly seemed to enjoy the experience.[10]

Volkswagen proved that a company can save a lukewarm relationship between its cult brand and its customers by committing the right amount of time and effort and by being honest. So can you and your own brand. We all make mistakes and have done things at one time or another that we later regret. The important thing is for the makers of cult brands to admit it to themselves when they've strayed off the beaten path and then take steps to rectify their problems. Look your best customers in the eye and tell them they're your most precious asset. And mean it. Customer congregations are a surprisingly forgiving bunch if your brand has the courage to speak from the heart.

 Cult brand companies are honest with themselves and realize their mistakes. No brand is infallible. A lukewarm relationship between your brand and its best customers is mendable. Can you be honest? Can you admit past mistakes? Try it and notice your customers' positive response.

Find the Way to Your Customers' Hearts

WWE's founding husband and wife team of Vince and Linda McMahon have always prided themselves on giving their customers what they want. When the couple first started their company, then called Titan Sports, they bought up a little known stadium in Cape Cod, Massachusetts, and started promoting all kinds of events there. Their first attraction was an exhibition hockey game featuring the NHL's Boston Bruins. To lure the Bruins for the match, the McMahons had to guarantee $50,000 in ticket sales up front, a huge number for the cash-strapped duo to come up with.[11]

The McMahons knew that they had to go all-out to promote the Bruins game. And go "all out" is exactly what they did. The McMahons created a VIP section packed with special perks, including homemade meatball sandwiches they actually made themselves before the game. Their plan worked. Fans were pleasantly surprised, the VIP section was a big hit, and the event ended up being the first in a long line of successful promotions run by the couple.

Perhaps just as important, this "make the customer happy at all costs" attitude is still clearly with the company today. The McMahons have not forgotten their "meatball sandwich" roots. World Wrestling Entertainment still understands the importance of listening to the choir. "You really have to be listening to them and providing them with what they want to see," says Linda McMahon, talking about WWE's legions of loyal fans. "I think that's really been the key secret to our success."[12]

WWE's live matches give the company a unique opportunity to see what its most loyal fans like or dislike about a show on any given night. Introduce a new wrestler or storyline twist that the crowd doesn't like, and chants of "Boooring! Boooring!" will soon follow. By the same token, if WWE hits upon a great new gimmick or introduces a cool new wrestler, their always vocal fans will definitely let them know about it. "One of the things about wrestling is that the fans feel that they are participating. Unlike in a sporting event, the fans *do* help determine the direction of wrestling," says Dave Meltzer, editor of the *Wrestling Observer* newsletter.[13]

"We look at 8,000 to 16,000 people in an arena on any given night as a huge focus group. We are able to test our ideas and see which of our superstars are fan favorites," adds Linda

McMahon.[14] Scripts often aren't fully set until the day of the show, and WWE will sometimes even change a script in mid-show based upon positive or negative fan reaction. In addition, WWE encourages fans to submit script ideas on its Web site.

The power WWE gains from preaching and listening to this choir of wrestling fanatics definitely isn't lost on Vince McMahon. "We're in contact with the public more than any entertainment company in the world," boasted McMahon in a *Fortune* magazine article.[15]

For those of you who are perhaps rolling your eyes at McMahon's last comment, McMahon doesn't just talk a good game; he backs it up. "At live shows, even when the TV cameras are turned off, sometimes Vince will give fans a bonus match or a twenty-minute skit with their favorite wrestler," says *Figure Four Weekly* newsletter editor Bryan Alvarez. "He always sends fans home happy."[16]

The reality is that every company, be it a hotdog vendor on the corner or the national grocery chain down the street, has the opportunity to go that extra mile for its customers each and every day. What it means to go this extra mile will vary by the type of business or industry, but you definitely know when you are—or aren't—doing it. Your customers do also. Remember,

 Cult brands do whatever it takes to send their best customers home happy. Does your company strive to accomplish this goal day in and day out? If not, why? Going the extra mile may be as simple as making tasty meatball sandwiches a la Vince and Linda McMahon.

there's a brand evangelist hiding somewhere deep inside all of us—cult branders just find creative ways to bring this loyalty to the surface. Do the unexpected for your customers, and the evangelists will follow.

You Need Brand Evangelists Just As Much As They Need You

Maybe your company has done great *without* any noticeable involvement from brand evangelists. Maybe you don't see any good reason to cultivate brand evangelists for your own product or service. Maybe you think brand evangelism is just a big waste of time and a fluffy, non-money-making idea cooked up by marketing kooks. After all, your business may already be successful, and things seemingly couldn't be better. But you'd be wrong—flat wrong. You need brand evangelists just as much as brand evangelists need you. Average companies may be able to skate by without them, but truly great companies *always* have them.

Have you ever stopped to think what having "home field advantage" in professional sports is really all about? Every sports team—be it the NFL's New York Giants or the neighborhood Pee Wee football team—would rather play its games at home than on the road. Why is this? Obviously, the playing field's dimensions are exactly the same from one stadium to the next, and the grass isn't magically greener at home than on the road. So what's the deal? Simple. The home team draws the most fans. The loyal crazy souls who will sit through rain, sleet, snow, and anything else Mother Nature can concoct just so they can root their team to victory.

For their part, the players on the home team feed off the almost electric energy and excitement these devoted fans, football's so-called "twelfth man," generate. The passion and cheers of a loud crowd have convinced many an underdog home team that it *can achieve* the impossible and come back from any deficit. In fact, many of the greatest upsets in sports history have happened with a favored visiting team losing because of a passionate home crowd. Cult brand companies react much the same way when they try seemingly crazy new ideas and dream the impossible dream. They can afford to take chances because they know they have dedicated brand evangelists in their corner.

Let's face it. Most people take bigger risks when they have the support of a group than when they're all by themselves. Thus, the encouragement and support of their loyal followers clearly help cult branders to adopt a "dare to be different" mindset. Would the New Beetle ever have been produced had it not been for the letters and calls of 35,000 fans? This outpouring of support clearly gave Volkswagen the courage to take a gamble. Or, would the original *Star Trek* series have ever made it into a third season if NBC hadn't received thousands of fan letters? It's doubtful. Brand evangelists help turn good companies into great companies.

 Never ignore an enthusiastic customer. Raving fans are never just a waste of time. Remember: You need brand evangelists just as much as they need you. Brand evangelists give you courage; they help you take risks and be a better brand. Embrace them!

Find Ways to Create Miracles for Your Brand Evangelists

As far back as the 1960s and the very beginning of the Internet, a sense of cooperation and brotherhood has always existed among computer programmers. Much like a group of academics in a university or researchers in a lab, programmers have always enjoyed sharing their work, in this case lines of computer code, amongst themselves. This attitude of sharing has produced a variety of grassroots computer programs that over time have crept into the mainstream. However, for all of this collaboration among the programmer community, as of 1990, computer geeks were still without a reliable and affordable operating system to "call their own."

There was already an operating system called UNIX that was widely used by engineers in universities and large corporations, but it was very expensive to run and wasn't intended at the time for low-powered desktop machines. What were these frustrated programmers supposed to do when they went home at night? These unhappy programmers were stuck with Windows 3.1 or DOS on their home PCs. Then, in 1991, Linus Torvalds, a twenty-one-year-old college student, set out to change this picture and develop what he called a "cheap alternative" to UNIX.[17]

You technical insiders know what happened next. In the summer of 1991, Torvalds posted on the Internet version 0.01 of the kernel for a new, free, powerful operating system that he called Linux. Within very little time, engineers around the world were sending Torvalds e-mails with snippets of new code for Linux. True to his academic roots, Torvalds had posted the entire source code for his operating system in full public view, and the programming community liked what they saw. With the wall down, they felt empowered. Within no time, a shy Torvalds found himself the ringmaster of the world's largest volunteer collaborative software effort with literally hundreds of contributors.

Today, Linux has millions of loyal users around the world, and Torvalds is rightfully treated as a near religious figure among fellow computer geeks. He has freed a nation of engineers from their chains to sub-par operating systems. Torvalds successfully tapped (or more likely stumbled) into the very essence of brand evangelism, and that's the lesson to take away from the Linux story for your own brand. Follow Torvalds' lead, and maybe you can tap into brand evangelism, too. Evangelists *need* to see miracles; they *need* their visions to become reality and their unexpressed needs to see the light of day.

When Torvalds decided to make Linux "open source" by letting anyone contribute code and keeping it free, he effectively laid the groundwork for just such a miracle. In the case of Linux, its brand evangelists weren't just making helpful suggestions about the product; *they were actually building it!* They could see, day by day, their thoughts and dreams in the form of lines of computer code actually being intertwined into the core of Linux. Piece by piece, they really were building an alternative to Windows.

Like any group of core followers behind a movement, revolution, religion, or cult brand, *the Linux community believed, and it was so.* Call it a gift or call it a miracle, but every cult brander needs to consistently offer the unexpected. No, that's not an oxymoron. Look at Linux again. Linus Torvalds stepped to the plate and gave the programming community something entirely *unexpected* to dream about and desire—a cheap but reliable alternative to UNIX. Then he did it all again, since Linux's collaborative nature allowed its followers to take part in this miracle, resulting in a further strengthening of their faith in the "Linux cause." Do the unexpected!

 We all want to believe, but first we need to see miracles in the form of unexpected gifts and surprises. Have you given your customers an unexpected gift that goes above and beyond what one would already expect from your product? Do something out of the ordinary. Think extraordinary.

Even When a Cult Brand Sins, the Choir Will Return to Church

Volkswagen is hardly alone as an example of a company with a long history of listening to its customers and then straying from its roots. Other companies have come just as close to falling into the abyss before they renewed relations with their vintage communities. In fact, some would argue that cult brand and teen shoemaker Vans Inc. also fell *into the abyss* for a few years before finding a way to crawl out. The Vans turnaround is an inspirational story for every brand holder looking to regain the faith and support of its choir of brand evangelists.

In the early 1980s, Vans' founder Paul Van Doren decided to step back from day-to-day involvement with his company. Bad move. Not content to stick with the existing "Vans formula," the new management team decided to drive the company into the vast new territory of manufactured and branded athletic shoes. Football, baseball, basketball, wrestling, soccer, skydiving, you name a mainstream sport or activity, and Vans began to make shoes for it. Not surprisingly, not only did the new lines of shoes put a financial strain on the company, they also began to erode its identity with its core brand evangelists, mainly teenagers who were into alternative activities like skateboarding and who shunned stuffy organized sports.

The result of these untimely moves was that Vans fluctuated in and out of bankruptcy for a few years until Paul Van Doren wisely took the helm again. Finally, in December of 1986, the company emerged from Chapter 11 and started battling back to respectability.[18] However, the company didn't really get its groove back until 1995. That's when Gary Schoenfeld took over from his father as CEO of Vans and laid the groundwork for the Vans of today. Gone was advertising in mainstream fashion publications like *GQ* and *Mademoiselle* that clearly must have alienated the Vans-wearing counter-mainstream skateboarders.[19]

To replace all this nonproductive advertising, Schoenfeld made an unexpected announcement of a major "gift" to the skateboarding community. Vans was going to create sanctioned championship events for its "core sports audience," the surfers, skateboarders, snowboarders, and BMX bikers. Vans was finally giving its core audience of brand evangelists the respect they deserved. Real cash purses. Real sponsors. Real exposure. Vans held its first major event, the World Championship of Skateboarding with Hard Rock Café, in October of 1995.[20] The next year, Vans became the title sponsor for the Warped Tour, an annual alternative music festival that travels to major U.S. cities.

Today, Vans sponsors a number of championship events in surfing, skateboarding, and BMX biking. All have gained wide respect and appreciation from the core sports community. The events demonstrate how much Vans really cares about its customers' lifestyles. Alternative bands and fans can't get enough of the Vans Warped Tour, which now draws over 400,000 attendees per year.[21] Vans has experienced record sales the past five years, and its core audience in the ten-to-twenty-four-year-old age group appears more loyal to the company's brand now than ever before.

Vans and Volkswagen demonstrate that the key to creating (or winning back) an evangelist for your brand is to do the unexpected. To go the extra mile. To create a miracle and to give a gift when your customer least expects it. Vans did this in spades through its festival and event sponsorships and is now reaping the rewards. The Vans choir is now firmly back in the church, and its "core sports" flock is again spreading the message. Make believers out of your own customers. Show them that your brand cares about their needs and desires, not just their wallets and pocketbooks. Win a customer's heart and mind and the rest will take care of itself.

 No one ever said that the battle to win a customer's heart and mind would be easy or wouldn't be frustrating at times. But the thinkers behind cult brands don't give up. They may fumble the ball, but they always stay in the game. The time to do the unexpected for your brand is *now*.

Rule 5

Cult Brands

Always Create

Customer Communities

I N 1982 AN American legend was close to giving up the ghost, and there seemed to be little that anyone could do to save it.

Milwaukee-based motorcycle manufacturer Harley-Davidson was teetering on the brink of financial ruin. A decade of brutal competition from Japanese motorcycle makers had taken its toll, and the company was truly between a rock and a hard place. To make matters worse, Harley was drowning in the debt incurred from the purchase of HD from industrial giant AMF the previous year. The deal allowed the Harley team to regain its independence but at a steep cost. Harley needed to get its sales back on track—fast!

Given Harley's financial condition, expensive traditional marketing was clearly out of the question. Partly with cost savings in mind, CEO Vaughn Beals announced in 1983 the launch of the Harley Owners Group, the factory-sponsored club for Harley owners mentioned in rule 2. He saw this as a grassroots way to reconnect Harley's brand and lifestyle with its most faithful customers. By forming H.O.G., Beals was hoping to create the foundation for local Harley "customer communities" around the country—and eventually the world.[1]

Although at first the H.O.G. concept didn't gain widespread acceptance, within a few years, dozens of H.O.G. chapters had sprouted around the nation. Thousands upon thousands of Harley riders became members. Beals and HD had hit a home run. This was truly guerilla marketing at its best. Harley generated initial membership in the owners group primarily from inexpensive promotions at dealerships and through word of mouth. The Harley nation became rock solid once again. Through H.O.G., Harley enthusiasts now had a structured way to meet, swap stories, and schedule rides with other evangelists.

Wisely, every local H.O.G. chapter had to have a local Harley dealership as its supporter and sponsor. The result of this stipulation was a tighter relationship between HD dealers and HD customers, as well as greatly increased motorcycle parts and merchandise sales for Harley. In one fell swoop, Harley had devised an ingenious way to give back to its customers and at the same time lay the groundwork for years of ongoing future revenue as part of the process. The creation of H.O.G. isn't the only reason that Harley survived its near ruin in the eighties, but "customer communities" certainly played an important role.

Harley's sagging reputation and balance sheet had both needed a major spark, and the Harley Owners Group clearly helped provide it. Says *Harley-Davidson Evolution Motorcy-*

cles author Greg Field, "The best way to grow revenue, other than by running sales, is to build a community. That's what they did through the Harley Owners Groups. Each one is basically tied to a Harley dealership."[2] Today, H.O.G. boasts over 640,000 members around the globe and is the largest factory-sponsored club in the world.

Has the H.O.G. story inspired you to start a company-run club or other membership concept for your own product or service? Great. However, Harley didn't stop with creating local clubs for its brand, and you and your company shouldn't either. You can do more. A lot more. Let's look into Harley's community push a little further. In addition to running the Harley Owners Group, Harley also organizes and helps underwrite the costs for hundreds of local and regional motorcycle rallies held each year for its faithful around the world.

Not only are the rallies great ways for the Harley community to congregate, they also represent a killer sales tool for the company. "Harley brings bikes with them to the rallies for people to try out. This is really big, because once people get on a new bike, that's all she wrote," says Daytona Beach H.O.G. member Sam Abrahamsen.[3]

Harley takes this "try-and-buy" concept to the next level twice a year in mega gatherings at Bike Week in Daytona Beach, Florida, and the Sturgis Rally and Races in South Dakota. Incredibly, the two multi-day events collectively attract over half a million bikers each year. Talk about mind-boggling numbers! That's enough motorcycle customers to fill up six huge football stadiums and still have some Hell's Angels to spare!

Of course, the big advantage of these blockbuster events for Harley is the unveiling of their hot new bikes and related merchandise. "At Bike Week each year, there are always examples of all the new bikes and every piece of clothing they make," says Harley rider Phil Jenkins. "So, anyone can look, see, feel, and touch all of the new bikes."[4] As any proud Harley-Davidson owner can tell you, all it takes is to hop onto a shiny new Harley bike, close your eyes, feel the power, dream a little, and chances are you're already sold. Harley shipped over 230,000 new bikes in 2001.

Besides Sturgis and Bike Week, Harley also throws a huge birthday bash celebrating the company's founding every five years at its Milwaukee headquarters. The celebration of Harley's 100-year anniversary in the summer of 2003 should be the company's biggest birthday party by far, with over 200,000 fans expected to attend the three-day festival.[5] A healthy serving of big-name live entertainment, food, merchandise displays, and of course, new Harleys are all scheduled for the massive event. HD promises its 100th anniversary celebration will be "the greatest party the world has ever seen." We don't doubt it.

Most companies can't spend nearly as much money on annual events and rallies as Harley does now that it has returned to prosperity. That's okay. What's important is that a company shows its customers it really cares about their business and wants its customers to regularly meet and mingle. If you're a small retailer, maybe this means holding a small birthday bash with free refreshments, food, and discounts once a year. Or, if you're a small service provider, what about holding a modestly sized special dinner for your best customers? Get creative. Satisfied customers want to get together. Show them the way.

Customer communities work. They make brands come alive. Plain and simple. In the case of Harley, its H.O.G. clubs helped save the company. Don't miss out on this huge opportunity to cost-effectively build lasting customer relationships and grow sales.

Star Trek's Organic Customer Community

While *Star Trek* producer Paramount has been criticized in recent years for not giving enough back to its fans, the reality is that the movie studio helped stimulate the creation of customer communities as long ago as the release of *Star Trek: The Motion Picture* over twenty years ago. The year was 1979 when a rabid eighteen-year-old Star Trek fan, Colorado teenager Dan Madsen, began publishing and distributing a small photocopied newsletter for fellow Trekkers.

"We ran the thing out of my basement. There were posters and all kinds of *Star Trek* stuff on the walls," Madsen recalled in an Associated Press article.[6]

Not on the ball at first, Paramount when it got wind of Madsen's Trekker newsletter approached him and accused him of copyright violations, even telling him he was violating the law. Soon thereafter, though, Paramount executives looked more closely at the content of Madsen's newsletters, saw he was really doing them a favor, and quickly brought him on board.

"We signed a contract with them. They thought it had the right amount of fanaticism and the right amount of professionalism they were looking for," added Madsen in the same AP piece.

Madsen's company has operated the Official Star Trek Fan Club and published the *Star Trek Communicator* magazine for over twenty years. The slick, four-color magazine now has over 30,000 subscribers and features interviews with the *Star Trek* cast, as well as behind-the-scenes looks at each of the shows. If you're a real hardcore Trekker, chances are you're a member of Madsen's club or have at least seen and read his magazine.

Now, let's look at all this from Paramount's perspective for a second. The Official Star Trek Fan Club and *Communicator* magazine are both excellent ways for *Star Trek's* movie company to inexpensively keep its fans around the world interested in the brand on a monthly basis. Plus, Paramount gets the benefit of the Official Star Trek Fan Club's evangelizing *without* having to roll up its sleeves and start preaching on its own. For his part, Madsen got to make a business out of something he loves. Thousands of fans around the world have a cool way to stay in touch with their favorite TV show. A true win-win for everyone involved!

 Look at your own customers. Do you already have a core group of rabid evangelists who would be interested in forming a club or writing a newsletter? We bet you do. Maybe they just need a little helping hand and guidance from your firm. Go find them and talk to them!

Use Marketing to Stimulate Your Customer Community

Jimmy Buffet's Margaritaville followed a path similar to Star Trek in creating its official customer communities. Scott Nickerson was a Sunshine State native who in 1989 had just recently moved from St. Augustine, Florida, to Atlanta, Georgia, to take a new job. In his new town Nickerson was feeling homesick. He began looking around Atlanta for friends who perhaps shared his same love for the Buffett island lifestyle. Soon after attending a Jimmy Buffett concert, the idea of forming a small, informal "Parrot Head Club" in Atlanta came to Nickerson. All he needed was the blessing of Jimmy Buffett's organization.

"Buffett's people asked me to write up the idea and send it to them," says Nickerson, "They were very supportive of it and said to go for it."[7]

Upon receiving approval from Buffett's Margaritaville team, Nickerson placed a small advertisement about the club in a local entertainment newspaper. The first meeting attracted only fourteen people. Within a few months, though, the club grew to dozens of members, and Nickerson's weekly happy hour gatherings were becoming very popular.

That's when Margaritaville Inc. really showed its marketing prowess and willingness to build customer communities, even if it did so partly by accident. Margaritaville promoted the idea of "Parrot Head Clubs" to all its fans in the *Coconut Telegraph,* a publication they distributed to customers on the Margaritaville Key West store's mailing list.

"When the first club started, a small blurb appeared about it in the *Coconut Telegraph,* which back then had only a few thousand subscribers," Nickerson recalls.[8]

Soon after reading about the clubs, Buffett fans around the country began contacting the Margaritaville store asking how they could start clubs in their local areas. Next thing Nickerson knew, he was sending out mini-business plans for starting Parrot Head clubs to dozens of fans. The Parrot Head nation had been born!

Today, Nickerson's small "Parrot Head Club" in Atlanta has evolved into a multi-national, nonprofit organization called Parrot Heads in Paradise, Inc. with chapter bylaws, a board of directors, and a national convention—the works! The club now has thousands of members in over 145 chapters, stretching from California to New York and from Mississippi to Michigan, plus international chapters in Australia and Canada.[9]

 We ask you again. Do you already have your own customer newsletter, magazine, or mailing list? Why not! Start one. How else do you plan on building an ongoing relationship with your fans? Don't let the opportunity to build your own customer community pass you by!

You Can Start Your Own Newsletter or Customer Community!

Publishing a regular newsletter or magazine for your customers doesn't have to be a multimillion-dollar undertaking. With a little creative thinking, you can develop and grow a publication quite inexpensively. For an inspirational example, look again at Jimmy Buffett and the *Coconut Telegraph*. As part of a plan to sell more Caribbean memorabilia and T-shirts, Buffett began issuing the publication from his cramped Key West Margaritaville store in February of 1985. It was not fancy, and the first issue went out to only 650 readers.[10]

Later that same year, though, the crafty Buffett released a new album. With it he provided an entry form for a "Last Mango Cruise" that would take five couples on an all-expenses-paid trip to Key West. The trip included a private concert by Buffett with, of course, unlimited margaritas and lots of cheeseburgers. In other words, a veritable heaven for Parrot Heads and a unique chance to meet their hero! When over 75,000 Parrot Heads entered the contest, Buffett used the names to grow a gigantic mailing list for the *Coconut Telegraph* virtually overnight. Jackpot!

Be like Buffett. If the star of your product or your service is your customers (and they should be!), then what better way to reward them and give back to them than by sponsoring a small event or holding a customer appreciation celebration? Or, what about something as simple as giving away free movie tickets or a small gift certificate? Holding community activities and stimulating the growth of communication vehicles like newsletters and clubs help make your brand more human. It shows that you care and aren't just some faceless money-grubbing corporation.

 When was the last time you held a contest with a prize or reward that your customers actually cared about? Everyone has dreams that they have a deep need to fulfill. What are the dreams of your customers? Create promotions that can fulfill their fantasies! And, oh yes, find a way to create your own mailing list of brand evangelists!

Create a Mecca for Your Customer Community

Build a church for your customers. That's right. Every cult brand needs and has its own Mecca. Pick any structured religion, organization, or movement, and they all have one or more significant meeting places. While these places might be Vatican City for Catholics and Wrigley Field for Chicago Cubs fans, every group has its own focal point for regularly meeting, socializing, and strengthening their "faith." The size and scale of this Mecca isn't nearly as important as the fact that your brand has one!

Never underestimate the power of having your own church-like focal point. This could be your company's factory, your first retail store, or even the home (or garage!) of your company's founder. You just need a place where you can continually revitalize your brand's faithful. Every cult brand needs a Mecca. Original Key West Margaritaville employee Cindy Thompson still recalls fondly the way Parrot Heads reacted upon first entering Jimmy Buffett's wildly popular store. "It always tickled me how people would walk in and go, 'Wow, I'm here!' It was like their Mecca. They had finally arrived," says Thompson.[11]

The concept of building and developing a moveable Mecca definitely wasn't lost on the folks at WWE. Since 1985, WWE has held its annual WrestleMania event in various locations around the country and has always enjoyed tremendous success. As recently as 2001, nearly 68,000 fans piled into the Astrodome in Houston, Texas, for WrestleMania 17. Wrestle-Mania is truly Woodstock for wrestling fans. All of the top names in WWE compete each year, and the storylines of many of WWE's matches all culminate in final high-profile showdowns at this blockbuster event.

For many wrestling fans, attending WrestleMania in person is a lot like having died and gone to heaven. It is the annual culmination and fulfillment of their true devotion to their cult brand, WWE. "WrestleMania was a great idea. Wrestling fans wanted their own version of the World Series and the Super Bowl, so that's just what Vince McMahon did," quips wrestling commentator Court Bauer.[12]

In 1994, the WWE decided to further reward its fans with the launch of WWE Fan Axxess, essentially a "fan festival" held prior to each WrestleMania. The festival has grown significantly over the past few years and today features autograph signings with dozens of WWE superstars, tons of exhibit booths filled with official WWE merchandise for sale, and interactive areas such as a life-size wrestling ring and a broadcast booth for fans to become "play-by-play" announcers.

What better way to fulfill WWE fans' fantasies than to have them hop into the ring and practice body slams and pile drivers or to see up close and personal a demolished car used in one of WWE's most recent TV skits! This is a tremendous way for WWE to reward its fans and also find ways to profit. Think about how you can get your own customers to become more up close and personal with your brand. WWE CEO Linda McMahon sums up her company's thinking behind Fan Axxess: "We really wanted to turn the WrestleMania weekend into a real experience for the fans," she says. "Our fans can never get enough of being up close and personal with their superstars!"[13]

The WWE took another important step in developing its customer community in September of 2000 when it opened WWE New York at New York's Times Square. The location features a 600-seat restaurant, an interactive game area, and a retail store. Most important, WWE New York includes a soundstage for TV production and live entertainment. Smartly, WWE regularly tapes portions of its TV shows at the New York location, putting restaurant goers in the middle of the action and giving fans another opportunity to interact with WWE superstars.

Okay, so not many companies can afford to hold spectacular events in sports arenas or have a restaurant in Times Square. But all companies can show their customers they really care. Every business—no matter its size—can find cost-effective ways to help its best customers regularly congregate. Don't use the excuse "Customer communities are too expensive to build." Savvy makers of cult brands will find a way. They know that satisfied customers respond better to a heavy dose of tender loving care than to a bucket of cash. Regular TLC shows that *you* care and that your customer's business really *does* mean something to you.

 Show your love for your customers. Spread your love for your customers. Create your own fan festival. Oh, you don't have one. Why? What are you waiting for? It doesn't have to be expensive. Every company can afford to have an annual customer appreciation day!

Apple Computer is a perfect example of how a heavy helping of TLC can trump a fat corporate checkbook any day of the week. Since the early eighties, Apple has been very supportive of its Mac User Groups, those essentially independent clubs lo-

RULE 5: **Cult Brands Always Create Customer Communities**

Cult Brands "Giving Back" in Action

Vans—Creates skate parks and hosts event for its customers
Mac—Sponsors and supports Mac User Groups around the world
WWE—Adjusts its show scripts based upon fan reactions during the match
Harley-Davidson—Sponsors regional rallies and local H.O.G. groups
VW—Created the New Beetle after receiving thousands of fan letters and calls
Star Trek—Opened "Star Trek: The Experience" in Las Vegas for its fans
Oprah—Uses viewer donations to support charities and worthy causes
Buffett—Reserves special concert tickets for Parrot Head club members
Linux—Hosts InstallFest parties to educate new users about Linux

Do you really listen to *and reward* your best customers? Cult branders are passionate about "giving back" to their customers with special gifts and unexpected surprises. A hearty dose of tender loving care—not millions of dollars worth of cheap marketing gimmicks—is the real way to win your customers' hearts. Think love first. Quick profits are for hucksters.

cated around the world started by Apple aficionados. Interestingly, Apple has historically provided these clubs with a speakers bureau, product information, training, and other helpful resources, but it has never really sunk a boatload of cold hard cash into them. Apple's real commitment to these groups has been thousands of hours of time and effort.

"The Mac User Groups were run by the users, but we gave them an incredible amount of support. When I was there, I would go out and meet with the user groups whenever I could," says former Apple CEO John Sculley.[14]

Think about the powerful and uplifting effect that Sculley's visits to the Mac faithful must have had at the time. Here is the CEO of one of the world's largest computer makers going around the country and taking time to press the flesh with ordinary folks who buy his products. This is what giving back to your customers is really all about!

Not only has Apple done a masterful job through the years with its Mac User Groups, it has also been excellent at maximizing its customer congregation opportunities—be it an important trade show or its annual shareholders meeting. Remember, most companies have only a limited number of opportunities each year to electrify and re-energize the faithful followers of their brands. So make yours count. Apple did this even in its earliest years by using the "Mecca" of its jam-packed shareholders meetings as the magical "unveiling points" for new product launches that were almost "ritualistic" in nature.

"We used to always use the annual shareholders meeting as the launch event for a new product. This started before I even got to Apple," says Sculley, who joined the company to much fanfare as its CEO in 1983 after previously serving as the head of Pepsi.[15]

In later years, Apple developed its Apple Expo and Macworld conventions into much more than typical trade shows. These conventions give Apple fans the opportunity to get up close and personal with Apple's hottest developers and newest products, as well as a rare chance to break bread with other Mac customers from all around the world. Apple takes these two events incredibly seriously and works hard to build media buzz around them. Says former Apple VP of Communications Christopher Escher, "We marked our calendars by the high

 Do you take every opportunity you can to regularly press the flesh with your best customers? How do they know you really appreciate them? When was the last time you picked up the phone and said to them those two simple words: Thank you?

holy days of Macworld and Apple Expo. These were the gatherings of the faithful."[16]

Some skeptics reading this chapter may be thinking that Mac User Groups might work great for Apple, and Harley Owners Groups might be fantastic for Harley, but "customer communities will never fly with my product or service. My company will never take this idea seriously!" Most probably, these skeptics have some financial types breathing down their necks and screaming for "instant profits." If so, you have to make it clear to the bean counters that the benefits of becoming a cult brand don't always happen overnight. Maybe you should tell them how shoe manufacturer Vans Inc. handled this.

Before Vans Inc. evolved into a global lifestyle brand, it was one small store in Anaheim, California. On its opening day in 1966 it had only three styles of rather ordinary, non-custom shoes to offer its customers. What's more, although the store's walls looked like they were stacked with tons of shoe-boxes, the reality was that all the boxes were empty! Vans' founder Paul Van Doren didn't even have enough money to manufacture that many shoes! Here was a case of a fledgling company that needed to start giving back to its community and spreading love to tons of customers it didn't even have yet—fast and cost-effectively. Not an easy challenge to overcome by any means!

What Vans did in the next decade to grow and reward its customer base as well as build good will in its community, all on a shoestring budget, is a lesson we should all take to heart. Vans put together a team of skateboarders that traveled around the schools in Southern California, putting on "safety" shows about skateboarding. At the time, parents were rightly concerned about the apparent safety risks involved with the new sport. Vans put on the safety shows for two reasons: to give back to its community and to prime its young customer base and their parents for future Vans' shoe sales.

"When we got the connections to get into the school system and start doing the safety shows, we reached a hell of a lot of kids back in the day," adds Everett Rosecrans, one of Vans' earliest employees and a member of Vans' original traveling safety team.[17]

Over time, the Vans' skate team began to appear at amusement parks across Southern California and big regional events like the Los Angeles Fair. To add some icing to the cake, Vans even paid for a free hour of skateboarding at local skate parks for buyers of their shoes. "It was just another incentive to buy a pair of Vans," says Rosecrans.[18]

 Okay. Now you see how you can indeed build your own customer congregation and give back to the local community, all on a shoestring budget. So what kind of educational programs and events should you be developing? Think small–but smart–like Vans. And then get moving!

Put a Ribbon Around Corporate Giving

It goes without saying that the world is indeed a better place because of the corporate giving that has become increasingly popular in recent years. Virtually every major corporation now makes regular donations to charities and nonprofit organizations, many of them desperate for funding. But where is the "halo effect" that many companies strive to achieve for their brands through gift giving? The good-guy image they're hoping for can sometimes look hypocritical in the light of highly publicized financial scandals and other business community disasters. Let's face it. Writing big checks isn't always the answer to creating a customer community! Writing checks is too easy. And consumers know it.

Perhaps there's a little something to learn about corporate giving from Oprah Winfrey's Angel Network. The talk show queen launched the Angel Network in September of 1997 with the goal of inspiring people to really "use their lives" and reap the rewards that come from giving to others. In Winfrey's words, "You get from the world what you give to the world. I promise this will change your life for the better."[19] It's hard to argue with the results. Through the donations of viewers, Oprah's Angel Network has now given homes to thousands of needy people and college scholarships to hundreds of deserving students.

Why has the Angel Network been such a huge success? There are many reasons, but first and foremost, Oprah has intimately involved her viewers in the gift-giving process. She makes it a two-way street. She not only writes checks to charities herself, she gets her fan base involved in the "giving-back" process right along side her. When the beneficiaries of the Angel Network's donations appear as guests on the *Oprah Winfrey Show*, viewers can see and almost feel the good that they are doing through this program.

Whether you like or dislike Oprah, you can't argue with the fact that she really does care for people whom she feels are "improving the lives of others." In fact, the Angel Network rewards these notable individuals with "Use Your Life" awards on the show. This is powerful stuff. The halo effect that the Oprah brand receives from these community activities is very real. We all feel a certain warmth and quiet joy from helping others. Brands that bring about these feelings in us will almost always hold a special place in our hearts.

Cult brands find ways to touch people's lives on a regular basis. Oprah's Angel Network does this masterfully. Why doesn't your own company get its customers involved in a gift-giving program? Your customers will love you for it, and your brand will benefit!

Maybe starting a program similar to Oprah's Angel Network isn't really "you" or wouldn't fit well with your product or service. In that case, there are other ways your brand can give back to your community and help your brand's image. WWE, for example, chose the presidential election year 2000 to launch its Smackdown Your Vote! initiative. WWE worked with a range of nonpartisan organizations and encouraged young people to get into the political process and vote.

In addition to promoting the program on its Web sites and TV shows, WWE had superstar wrestler and Olympic gold medalist Kurt Angle register young people to vote at his WWE book signings around the country. And register they did. When all was said and done, WWE's Smackdown Your Vote! helped register 150,000 new voters in the two months before the election.[20] Given the incredible closeness of the 2000 U.S. presidential race, a WWE-inspired new voter may have ended up casting the deciding ballot in the hotly contested election. Who would have thunk it?

Whether WWE *really* impacted the election or not, it was rewarded with a significant amount of positive press coverage for the program. Even more important, the initiative helped convince parents of young wrestling fanatics that the folks at WWE weren't really so bad after all, that they had a heart and were good citizens. Even though their wrestling matches may have been violent and over-the-top at times, they clearly cared about government and getting people to vote. Heck, WWE superstar The Rock even showed up and spoke at the Republican National Convention in 2000. All smart moves.

Apple Computer has never sponsored a "get out the vote" initiative or launched a high-profile, nonprofit operation like Oprah's Angel Network, but it has created buckets of goodwill through the years by its donations to students and educators. Education is where Apple really gives back. For nearly 25 years, Apple has devoted significant resources towards helping teachers and students in the classroom. Their generosity has paid off. Although Apple's share of the overall PC market now sits in the mid to low single digits, Apple reigns as the number two player in the education market after Dell Computer.

Without a doubt, Apple would today only be a niche player in the educational market if many years ago CEO Steve Jobs had not decided to concentrate on programs and products that help students learn. This plan worked. School administrators can see and feel that Apple and Jobs care about the educational community and have responded accordingly.

As Jobs proclaimed at an education conference in 2001, "We're in education not just because we want to make revenue and profits, although that's important, but because we give a damn, just like you guys."[21] Yep. Apple gives a damn, and its brand benefits from this!

The WWE helps recruit voters. Apple focuses on serving educators and students. What can your company do that will leave a positive impact on the community? Can you improve the local government or library or schools? Sure you can. Ask your customers how.

Cult Brands

Are Inclusive

MADISON AVENUE has it all dreadfully wrong. The ad guys have been trying to convince us for years that great brands are built upon product exclusivity and targeted marketing. The more targeted and exclusive the brand, the better. Like sheep, many large companies—just look at a big chunk of the Fortune 500—have bought into this strategy. Print and broadcast advertising copy for many major brands is now peppered with both direct and subliminal messages proclaiming their exclusivity. Our e-mail boxes, mailboxes, magazines, and TV sets overflow with this same message. Exclusive offers. Exclusive products or services. Exclusive memberships. Exclusive opportunities. All highly targeted, of course!

The world is full of marketers hellbent on microtargeting their brands' marketing messages and attributes only to select audiences. What does this mean? Imagine your brand targeting small bites—not even slices—of the overall consumer pie, and that gives you a good idea of Madison Avenue's current "success formula." Slice and dice your brand's target audience now, ask questions later. While we shake our heads in amazement at this kind of behavior, these marketers are proud as punch that they have created a niche for their new brand and made it as exclusive and inaccessible to the general public as possible.

The more exclusive a product or service seems, the thinking goes, the more desirable and attractive it will supposedly become to the targeted consumers. Put another way, these are the same marketers that all too happily carry around imaginary profiles of their "perfect customer" as a badge of honor, as if they are delighted their brand is not for sale to the unwashed masses. It is special, segmented, and snooty. How laughable. Regrettably for Madison Avenue, this is a brand-building strategy that often crumbles miserably. Hypothetical spreadsheets and customer databases don't create cult brands!

Be assured that marketers of cult brands don't target imaginary perfect customers with "exclusive" products. Cult branders sell real products to real customers that fulfill real wants and needs. Think Joe and Jane Consumer. While one-to-one targeted marketing and computer-driven demographic profiling and analyses are wonderful and valuable inventions, they have little or nothing to do with real brand building or maintaining customer loyalty. That's why the marketers of cult brands laugh at the very notion of exclusivity. Unless you're a luxury goods company, inclusiveness—not exclusiveness—should be your brand's primary mission and battle cry.

> Don't let your brand fall into the bottomless pit of exclusivity and myopic targeting. Segmenting your audience and building imaginary profiles of your perfect customers may seem useful, but these tasks do little to build lasting customer loyalty. Smart brands are inclusive.

Cult Brand Customers Range in Age from Eight to Eighty

Get out into the field and look at a cult brand's typical customers. Visit and walk the floor of a Star Trek convention. Go to a Jimmy Buffett concert. Have a cup of coffee with some Harley-Davidson owners. Talk to some Linux or Macintosh fanatics. Even check out a WWE wrestling event when it comes to your town. This is probably the most valuable (and most fun!) marketing research you'll ever get a chance to do. At the end of the day, you'll more than likely come up with the conclusion that cult brands are all incredibly open and inclusive companies. In fact, their customer bases are so diverse that their followers generally cut across all ages, races, genders, creeds, and socioeconomic backgrounds.

Why do cult brands like Star Trek, Jimmy Buffett, Linux, Apple, and WWE all have customers that range in age from eight to eighty? Simple. Don't forget that cult branders aren't just selling a product or a service; they are selling the opportunity to fulfill their customers' passions, dreams, and aspirations. The need for feelings of self-empowerment and self-fulfillment is timeless and ageless. These are universal qualities that all human beings share. A rebellious young teenager and an aging baby boomer, while separated in decades by age, both want the same feelings of temporary escapism and unrestricted fun that seemingly only Jimmy Buffett's island-lifestyle-inspired concerts and music can provide.

A great cult brand like Harley-Davidson would likely have never got off the ground and recovered fabulously in the late eighties if it had fallen into the trap of brand exclusivity and nearsighted targeting. Can you imagine what would have happened if Harley had started running ads and sponsoring events geared only toward single blue-collar males living in rural markets with a median household income of $30,000 to $35,000 a year? While it's hard to predict the outcome of a hypothetical future, if Harley *had* followed this strategy, it likely would have out-marketed and outsmarted itself right out of hundreds of thousands of loyal new "weekend riders."

A peek into the Harley nation today reveals thousands upon thousands of middle-aged lawyers, doctors, accountants, and other upwardly mobile professionals happily coexisting with long-time blue-collar Harley owners. In short, the Harley nation is now as diverse as a cross-section of the entire American population, and for good reason. What Harley is ultimately selling through its motorcycles is the opportunity to experience the feelings of raw freedom and empowerment that one receives from strapping on some leather and riding a bike down an open road. These are feelings common to Americans of *all* ages, races, and backgrounds.

By the same token, where would Vans shoes be today if Vans' founder Paul Van Doren had opened his first store in California with the intention of building an exclusive brand that only served customers with a distinct psychographic profile? It's possible Vans might not even be around today. Instead, Paul Van Doren built a brand that was inclusive from the start. His original dream was simply to manufacture shoes and sell them directly to the public. As such, any customer, regardless of age or background, was a good customer in Van Doren's mind. With this practical philosophy, Vans was very open to catering to the wants and needs of Southern California skateboarders (then viewed as social outcasts) when they began buying his shoes in the mid-seventies. In effect, these skateboarders found Vans shoes, Van Doren didn't target or "find" them.

 Cult brand manufacturers are incredibly open and inclusive. In fact, exclusivity and targeting aren't even in their vocabulary. Are you surprised that many cult brand companies have customers that range in age from eight to eighty? Don't be. Cult brands fulfill feelings that are timeless and ageless.

Cult Brands Are Universal

It's hardly by accident that Oprah Winfrey has maintained such a fervently steadfast and devoted fan base during her career. For over fifteen years now, she has used the *Oprah Winfrey Show* as a daily platform for holding heart-to-heart discussions with her audience. While some TV personalities seem distant and removed from the general public, Oprah has never shied away from sharing intimate personal details about her life with

her audience. Oprah has openly discussed such incredibly difficult and personal topics as being raped at nine years old and
using cocaine in her twenties, as well as her ongoing high-
profile battle with obesity.[1]

By sharing these intimate personal details, Oprah shows
her viewers that when the lights and cameras are all put away
she faces many of the same problems as they. She is indeed
an *ordinary person* with *ordinary problems* to overcome. It's
her seeming vulnerability and fragility that make her that
much more of an inclusive brand. As Dennis Swanson, the television executive who hired Winfrey in 1983 to host *A.M.
Chicago,* told the *New York Daily News:* "There's a vulnerability about Oprah. She was a black female in what was at the
time a white, male-dominated business. She was overweight.
She wasn't famous."[2]

Singer-songwriter and cult brander Jimmy Buffett has taken
a similar approach to building a sense of inclusiveness and
openness between his brand and his fans. While Buffett has
never shared as many intimate details about his life as Oprah
has, he has written songs for over twenty-five years that have a
lasting and timeless allure. Buffett's light-hearted tales of fish-
ing, sailing, relaxing, and partying in exotic tropical destinations represent places, attitudes, and escapes that people of *all*
ages and *all* backgrounds fantasize about. At their core his
songs reflect more a person's "state of mind" than a particular
age or background.

Buffett's concerts are today filled with everyone from aging
baby boomers who have listened to Buffett for decades to
teenagers who have just recently discovered his music. Buffett's

songs speak of experiences, fears, and desires that we *all* share as human beings. The lyrics to "Margaritaville," Buffet's trademark song, sum up the overall inclusive flavor of his music. As a 1998 article in the *Washington Post* noted: "The burnt-out hero of 'Margaritaville,' struggling valiantly to reconstruct an entire season unaccountably misplaced, could be *any* age, from 16 to 60."[3] Age, race, gender, and background are all irrelevant in Buffett's world of carefree escapism.

As for *Star Trek,* the TV series and movies have always had themes of openness and acceptance of all races, creeds, and nationalities. Let's not forget that the cast of the original TV series included a black female (Uhura), a Russian (Checkov), an Asian (Sulu), and even an "alien life form," the Vulcan Spock, all working together as the crew of the *U.S.S. Enterprise.* It doesn't get much more inclusive than that! Explains long-time *Star Trek* expert Richard Arnold, "*Star Trek* is about a future society where we have all survived with dignity. We don't all get killed by a huge bomb. Instead, we unite as a planet."[4]

Star Trek, Jimmy Buffett, and Oprah Winfrey each go about making their brands feel inclusive and open in slightly different ways, but they each achieve the same goal. Consumers of all ages, genders, races, creeds, and backgrounds feel comfortable buying and supporting these brands. These consumers feel not only wanted and appreciated by the owners of these brands, they can also fully relate to the values, ideals, dreams, aspirations, and experiences that the brands symbolize. How can your own brand become more inviting and open? What *universal* wants and needs does your brand satisfy for your customers?

Every company regardless of its line of business or the size of its bankroll can become more open and inclusive. Ask yourself these questions: What wants and needs does every human being have? Which of these universal wants and needs can my brand fulfill?

Cult Brands Have "Sharing" and "Collaboration" in Their Blood

Nothing lets a customer better know that a brand is truly inclusive than when the company listens *and acts* on the advice its customers give it. As human beings, we all get pleasure from sharing our thoughts, ideas, experiences, and discoveries with others, and we are naturally drawn to people and organizations that value and appreciate what each of us has to share. We are even more drawn to people and organizations that actually *take* our input and *act* upon it. Not surprisingly, the vast majority of cult brands all have a strong "sharing" and "collaborative" component associated with them.

This theme of collaboration and sharing is a prime driver behind the fiery passion and fierce loyalty that software developers have had for Linux for over a decade now. The open-source development process that the Linux operating system is built upon is a superb example of the power of openness and inclusiveness in practice.

"Part of the whole Linux community thing is: 'I know this, I'm willing to share it with you, you know that, you're willing to share that with me,'" explains Jon "Mad Dog" Hall, the Executive Director of Linux International and a leading advocate for open-source software.[5]

The core developers of Linux, like Linus Torvalds, understood from the beginning that we all love to share. And that we all love for people to listen *and then act* on what we have to say. It's not surprising at all that hundreds of thousands of developers around the world feel deep connections and genuine bonds with Linux and other Linux developers. Linux followers all feel universally welcome, loved, and appreciated. This is because they can actually *see* their own ideas and lines of software code at work in the Linux operating system. The open-source development process doesn't discriminate. As long as he or she writes good code, a developer's age, race, creed, or background doesn't matter in the Linux community.

"A lot of times, I don't know someone's race, age, or sexual orientation because I talk to them through e-mail," says Rob Malda, founder of Slashdot.org, a popular online haven for computer geeks. "It really doesn't matter, though, because it's more about if they can kick out a few thousand lines of code to back up what they say."[6]

In other words, "the best code" always wins in the Linux nation, whether it comes from a fourteen-year-old kid in Buenos Aires or a fifty-year-old veteran programmer working for a major U.S. corporation. While this competitive aspect of the Linux community might seem intimidating to an outsider, this performance-based world is actually refreshing for software developers, since they know they will be judged by their peers for the quality of their work and their ideas and not by their age, job title, background, or work experience. Call it

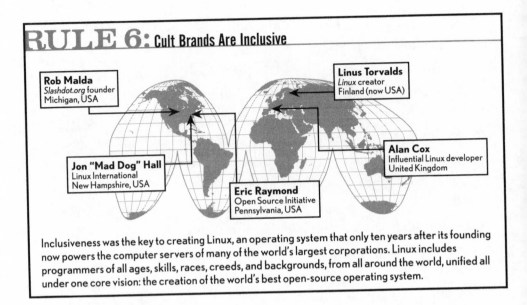

RULE 6: Cult Brands Are Inclusive

Rob Malda
Slashdot.org founder
Michigan, USA

Linus Torvalds
Linux creator
Finland (now USA)

Jon "Mad Dog" Hall
Linux International
New Hampshire, USA

Alan Cox
Influential Linux developer
United Kingdom

Eric Raymond
Open Source Initiative
Pennsylvania, USA

Inclusiveness was the key to creating Linux, an operating system that only ten years after its founding now powers the computer servers of many of the world's largest corporations. Linux includes programmers of all ages, skills, races, creeds, and backgrounds, from all around the world, unified all under one core vision: the creation of the world's best open-source operating system.

"tough love" if you like, but for developers there isn't a more inclusive place than the Linux nation!

Cult brand and shoemaker Vans has also done an excellent job of building true collaboration and sharing between its brand and its customers. Time and again, Vans has proven to its customers that not only does it listen to their suggestions and value their input, it also actually *makes* their best ideas come true. The first company to really take the wants and needs of Southern California skateboarders seriously, it understood that skaters not only wanted shoes that looked "one of a kind" but actually *were* one of a kind. Vans collaborated with its customers by going into the custom shoe business after receiving numerous requests for funky-looking custom shoes from Southern California skateboarders.

"In the early seventies, Vans was famous because they made custom-made shoes. You could take fabric down to their store, and they would make you shoes right out of that fabric," recalls former pro skateboarding legend turned entrepreneur and movie director Stacy Peralta. "That was pretty much unheard of!"[7]

Today, Vans continues to stick to its inclusive message by actively seeking out and implementing new product ideas from the dozens of "core sports" athletes the company sponsors. But Vans hasn't stopped there at fostering a sense of "sharing" with its customers. The opening of numerous large Vans' skateboard and BMX-biking parks around the country in recent years has given the company yet another touch point for staying close to its customers. At the parks, Vans hears directly from its customers about what it's doing right with its products, what it's doing wrong, and how it can improve.

It's clear that Vans CEO Gary Shoenfeld is keenly focused on continuing to build an environment of collaboration and openness that connects the Vans brand with its customers. As Schoenfeld told *Inc.* magazine in 1999, "Our designers and product people spend a lot of time at the parks. We do some focus groups there, but we've found that we get the best insights when our people hang out with teens more informally. We also learn by watching them skate. As they push things in their sports and find ways to do new tricks, we can incorporate design changes into our footwear."[8]

 Learn to share! When was the last time you actually listened to your customers' suggestions and turned the best ones into reality? Nothing helps a brand become more open and inclusive than accepting, valuing, and incorporating its customers' ideas.

Cult Brands Abolish "Command-and-Control" Thinking

A company's employees can also be powerful secret weapons for building a genuine environment of sharing and openness between its brand and its customers. Unfortunately, far too many brand holders—ranging from monolithic Fortune 500 giants right down to small mom-and-pop corner shops—still stick with a command-and-control management style. The powers-that-be in these companies can't get over the mental hurdle that they're in charge, and they don't allow their employees to interact as real human beings with their customers. These brands almost invariably have salespeople and customer service reps who appear tethered to a painfully short leash.

You probably know this scenario all too well. We've all dealt with a company—maybe a department store, a car dealership, or an appliance megastore—whose well-intentioned employees clearly want to provide honest advice but can't. They come off sounding like robots spouting the company line. Invariably, this kind of experience leaves a nasty taste in our mouths about that company's brand. Instead of feeling appreciated and welcome, the customer feels frustrated and excluded. Are things this way for your own brand? Allow your employees to act and be human. Set them free. Empower them. Let them speak their minds.

What do you have to lose? What are you worried might happen? If your firm has a high-quality product or service, then employees who act and sound like real people when talking to customers can only help—never hinder—your brand. Cult branders never lose sight of the fact that enduring relationships are built upon truth and honesty. If you want your brand to create feelings of openness and inclusiveness with consumers, then you must set your employees free. Break down the command-and-control walls. Unleash your employees' honesty and fairness. Encourage them to sound and act more like human beings around customers instead of cold and detached purveyors of preprogrammed marketing drivel.

Harley-Davidson demonstrates beautifully a company whose employees are not only free of command-and-control shenanigans but are actually encouraged to mix and mingle with customers. The results are impressive. Today, literally hundreds of Harley employees—from factory workers up to senior executives like CEO Jeffrey Bleustein—attend many of Harley's major motorcycle rallies and gatherings around the country. At virtually any one of these rallies one invariably finds Harley executives and employees rubbing elbows, swapping stories, and hanging out with fellow Harley riders.

Harley takes the feedback its employees receive at these events very seriously. As Bleustein explained in a 1996 interview with *@issue: The Journal of Business & Design,* "A lot of what you see in our product lines—and even the way we run our rallies—are the direct result of input that we've received from our customers."[9]

The Bleustein formula is simple but potent: Harley listens—and then *acts*—on the wants and needs of its customers. Harley encourages its employees to freely socialize with its customers. Have a few beers. Swap tales and build real friendships. Is it at all surprising that Harley owners feel such a strong fondness and loyalty to the HD brand? Of course not. In a world where so many companies are stuck in command-and-control land, brands like Harley that have switched on the light between customer and employee shine even that much brighter!

As consumers, we want more brands that honestly value our suggestions and genuinely appreciate our business. We're tired of snooty brands that take us for granted or refuse to make our lives any better or easier. Far too many companies make us feel like statistics, and we're absolutely sick of it! What we like are brands from companies that make a genuine effort to get to know us as living, breathing human beings and not just bunches of tiny numbers on an Excel spreadsheet.

That's why consumers can't help but be drawn to a cult brand like Harley-Davidson, which has proven time and again that it honestly values feedback and suggestions from its customers. As Harley Vice President of Styling Willie Davidson, affectionately known as "Willie G" among fellow riders, noted in the same *@issue:* article, "The rallies like the ones in Sturgis or Daytona Bike Week really serve as our product development centers. We see thousands of bikes and what our customers are doing to them. We get new ideas through our discussions. And then the riders take demo rides on our new models and give us feedback."[10]

Any company can follow Harley's path of being friendly and open with its customers. It will take time, effort, and commitment from you and your employees. Follow through with these steps, though, and increased brand loyalty will invariably be in your future. If you are a little in doubt about setting your employees free, think for a minute about a shop or restaurant where you go on a regular basis mostly because you've become friendly and familiar with one or more of the employees. This is human nature at work. Remember: People want to do business with other people that they like, not with some faceless, unapproachable corporation. So put a face to your brand. Let your employees become real people.

The days of managing the relationship between your employees and your customers with an iron grip are over. Tear down your command-and-control "iron curtain" between the two if you haven't already. Give your brand a friendly face. Set your employees free!

Use Advertising to Convey Openness and Inclusiveness

Beyond "sharing" with its customers and setting its employees free, there is another way a brand can become more inclusive, and that is through advertising. Your brand's advertising can either enhance your overall message of openness and inclusiveness or it can tear this message to pieces. Few things hurt a brand worse than an advertising campaign that conveys a different marketing message from how the product or service "walks, talks, and acts" in reality.

Make sure this kind of disconnect in communication never happens to your brand. Before you launch any new advertising campaign, always ask yourself this one question: Do these ads convey a message that my brand is open, friendly, and inclusive? Analyze the marketing plan behind any cult brand and you'll often find that every facet of its advertising from print and TV ads all the way down to its in-store displays gives off a feeling of openness and friendliness. These ads all focus intently on demonstrating that *anyone* and *everyone* is welcome to use the company's product or service. No one is left out.

It is hardly an accident, for example, that every issue of Oprah Winfrey's O magazine features a smiling photo of Oprah on its cover. Sure, Oprah is the brand people are "buying into" when they purchase a copy of O, but the reason Oprah is on the cover goes much deeper than that. Study the rack of women's magazines next time you are in a bookstore. Pick up a copy of O, and you'll see that Oprah's cover photo is always warm, friendly, and approachable. She creates a stark contrast to the tall svelte models with seemingly impossible body dimensions on the covers of many other women's magazines. Oprah's inclusiveness wins out over the other magazines' exclusiveness.

Cult brand car manufacturer Volkswagen is another company that effectively uses advertising to deliver its message of family and inclusiveness. While the vast majority of car manufacturers design their new models to sell to a particular segment of the car-buying public, Volkswagen has largely refused to go down this path. And for good reason. Trying to use demographics and psychographics to develop a profile of the ideal Beetle buyer is wasted effort, because the lifestyle, attitude, and dream a Beetle fulfills defies age, race, gender, and socio-economic background.

Wisely, for the launch of the New Beetle in 1998, Volkswagen made a conscious decision *not* to show any actual "drivers" in magazine or television ads. VW wanted its funky shaped and lovable little car—not an actor or actress—to be the center of the public's attention. "In the New Beetle's initial advertising, we never included people in the ads because we didn't want a person to say, 'Oh, that's who drives a Beetle,'" explains Steve Keys, Director of Corporate Communications for Volkswagen of America. "We wanted you to be able to say, 'I can see myself in that car.'"[11]

Good move. The age range of buyers of the New Beetle included everyone from teenagers buying their first car to aging baby boomers hoping to recapture their youth. No one had trouble seeing themselves sitting behind the wheel of a New Beetle! Clearly, VW benefited from not artificially shrinking its potential audience of buyers. The fact that Volkswagen's initial "no-people" advertising strategy for the New Beetle worked certainly hasn't gone unnoticed by other automotive companies and ad agencies. In particular, Daimler-Chrysler's advertising for its new PT Cruiser and Prowler models has taken the same "no-driver" approach.

Perhaps because it's the ultimate lifestyle brand, Harley-Davidson also generally never shows people in its ads. Check out any Harley TV or print ad, and you'll rarely see people on the bikes. What you will see is a shiny Harley-Davidson standing alone on a picturesque open road just waiting for someone to ride it off into the sunset. As Ken Schmidt, Harley's Director of Communications, told *@issue: The Journal of Business and Design* about this strategy, "The idea is that with a Harley-Davidson, you can be anyone you want to be."[12]

 Advertising can make or break your efforts to make your brand more open and inclusive. Keep in mind that cult brand advertisements consistently reinforce the notion that *anyone* and *everyone* is always welcome to use their products and services.

Cult Brands Sell "Unfinished Finished Products"

The genius of cult brand holders is that they allow individuals to join forces and form a group identity, while still preserving and celebrating individuality. One way they do this is by providing "unfinished finished products." This expression comes from Richard Teerlink, former CEO at Harley-Davidson, who views all Harley bikes as vehicles that "people can mold into their own."[13] To further this concept, Harley has stepped up the customization of its bikes in recent years, and now has a whopping 720-page parts-and-accessories catalog.[14]

Independent companies and designers have always enjoyed a sizeable aftermarket as specialists in customizing Harleys. Then, a few years ago, Harley began selling its own highly customized bikes directly to customers. It's a case where everyone wins. Consumers who buy a custom Harley feel like they are not only joining the "Harley nation" as a whole but that they are also exercising their own individuality. For Harley-Davidson, offering custom bikes means the company can rack up juicier, higher-margin sales. This is both inclusiveness and openness at work as well as good old-fashioned capitalism.

Another "unfinished finished product" is the Volkswagen Beetle, arguably the most customized car in the world. The popular notion that no two Beetles are exactly alike probably isn't that much of a stretch. Volkswagen as a company has never been particularly aggressive at pushing customization of the Beetle, but as is the case with Harley, an independent aftermarket has thrived for years customizing the car for Beetle owners. Next time you are out driving, pay particular attention to any Beetles you see. Look for some little touch of personality the owner has added. You'll likely find it!

It's not just transportation companies like Harley-Davidson and the Beetle, though, that have successfully created "unfinished finished products." Cell phone giant Nokia has proved that even a mass-produced consumer electronics device like the cell phone can still express individuality. Nokia ingeniously offers dozens of snap-on covers, screen savers, and downloadable ringing tones so its customers can personalize their phones. Look at your own business. The opportunity to build an "unfinished finished product" for your customers is likely already there. Help your customers express themselves!

 Makers of brands like Harley-Davidson, the Volkswagen Beetle, and Nokia are all experts at building "unfinished finished products." How can you make your own product or service more customizable and personalizable?

Rule 7

Cult Brands Promote Personal Freedom and Draw Power from Their Enemies

I T'S TIME to dust off your old Western Civilization and American History textbooks from school. Pull them out of your closet, the basement, your attic, or wherever else you've stowed away and forgotten all your old mementos of higher learning. Go to the bookstore if you must. No kidding. You'll be glad later. Start rereading the Declaration of Independence, the U.S. Constitution, and the Bill of Rights while you're at it. If you're *really serious* about becoming a top-notch cult brander, you'll *always keep in mind* what these historic documents are all about.

Why should you be so gung-ho about the message of American history and documents like the Declaration of Independence? Because they regularly remind us exactly what truly successful cult brands are "selling" to their customers day in and day out. A powerful dose of good old-fashioned freedom.

We all know that people live for freedom. People fight for freedom. Many people are willing to die for just a *chance* at freedom. No one likes to live under a dictatorship either in a nation or the consumer marketplace. No one.

For years, savvy cult branders have understood that consumers are actively looking for the opportunity to buy feelings of freedom in their everyday lives. Less restraint. Less control. More independence. These are the "products" that cult brands often help provide. Admittedly, cult brands are not selling the same freedom the American colonists were seeking when they broke away from the British monarchy over two centuries ago, but they sell a very real and powerful theme of freedom nonetheless.

Anyone or anything that seemingly attempts to curtail or take away our "freedom" we generally dislike. Nothing gets a group of Americans riled up more quickly than issues that relate to limiting freedom of speech or freedom of religion. Curiously, though, very few brands today (large or small) even *attempt* to capitalize on the huge thirst and need our society has for products and services that help reinforce this freedom theme.

Instead, we see marketers today who are hung up on promoting their product or service with tired catchphrases like *the best, the greatest, the quickest, the fastest, the longest lasting, bigger and better,* or *new and improved.* This "feature-benefit" marketing at the bottom of Maslow's pyramid is all fine and good, but it's hardly unique or eye-catching, and it does *nothing* to evoke consumers' ultimate need for feelings of freedom. The makers of cult brands don't make this mistake. Each and every one sells a unique kind of freedom tailored to the specific wants and needs of its customers.

Take a quick look at some examples. What theme of freedom is Jimmy Buffett selling to his Parrot Heads at his concerts, restaurants, and in his albums? How about temporary freedom from eight-to-five jobs, work deadlines, monthly bills to pay, and children to raise? The McMahons' WWE sells a similar blend of freedom. For a wrestling fan, watching a WWE television show or going to a live match is a great way to feel release from life's responsibilities for a few hours. Oprah's fans receive temporary freedom from the daily grind when they watch her talk show or read her magazine.

Harley-Davidson also sells its customers an undeniably strong sense of freedom. What is more utterly freeing than riding a motorcycle down an open road with the wind in one's face! *American Iron* magazine editor Chris Maida is one of many Harley owners who told us that he absolutely "loves the freedom on two wheels" that he feels when he's riding a bike.[1] HD's fun-filled clubs and rallies provide Harley owners with a temporary freedom from their generally button-downed and regimented lives.

The people behind cult brands like Apple Computer and the Volkswagen Beetle sell a slightly different theme of freedom in addition to liberating their customers from the monotony of life. The Mac and the Beetle reinforce their customers' strong feelings of nonconformity. Both the Mac owner in 1984 and 2002 and the Bug owner in the sixties and today feel a certain "rebellion against authority" in owning these products. Both brands make people feel they're more independent than the masses who make up the "mindless majority."

This theme of freedom from "totalitarian control" is also the basis of the powerful grassroots growth behind the Linux brand. While, ironically, many large corporations now use Linux software on their computer networks because it is faster, cheaper, and more reliable than the competition, the individuals who actually write the computer code have been drawn to the Linux phenomenon for an entirely different reason. Thousands of software developers around the world see Linux as an opportunity to regain control of their jobs and to put zest back into their creative juices.

"In the Linux world, we frequently cite Thomas Jefferson and Ben Franklin because they believed in the freedom of the individual," explains Bob Young, the cofounder of Red Hat, the world's largest distributor of Linux and open-source software. "It's almost like free speech. Software really is just a form of expression. There's a reason that software languages are called languages."[2]

The basis of the "open-source" philosophy behind Linux is a radical shift from popular "closed-source" programs like Microsoft's Windows. Makers of closed-source software don't freely share their source code—the underlying guts of a computer program—with third parties. They keep this code locked up, and other developers have to guess why a program isn't working properly and often have a hard time trying to fix its "bugs."

 Makers of cult brands keep an underlying theme of freedom running throughout their businesses. So, does your brand provide your customers with a healthy dose of good old-fashioned freedom? No one likes to feel owned or controlled. We enjoy breaking free. Help us all get there!

RULE 7: Cult Brands Promote Personal Freedom and Draw Power from Their Enemies

The Archenemy	The Cult Brand
"The history of the present King of Great Britain is a history of *repeated injuries* and *usurpations*, all having in direct object the establishment of an absolute *Tyranny* over these States. To prove this, let Facts be submitted to a candid world."	"We hold these truths to be self-evident, that *all men* are created equal, that they are *endowed by their Creator* with certain unalienable Rights that among these are *Life, Liberty* and the *pursuit of Happiness*."
—The Declaration of Independence	—The Declaration of Independence

The Founding Fathers were ingenious cult branders. They understood that *every* revolution must have a villain and that the best way to unify a group (in this case, thirteen colonies) was to highlight the archenemy's wrongdoings and opposing beliefs. The famous lines quoted above from the Declaration of Independence paint the battle lines between Freedom (cult brand) and Tyranny (arch-enemy) beautifully!

Cult Brands Create Lasting Memories

We all have enjoyable memories that we treasure forever in our minds. The images and sounds of a wedding ceremony. A baby's first steps. An important birthday party. Your child's college graduation. We cherish and hold these memories near to our hearts. We value these memories so much that we try to capture them and save them forever inside photo albums, personal diaries and journals, and videotapes. We like to share them with friends and family. Sometimes, we even erect monuments in remembrance of them.

Memories are part of each of us as individuals. Without memories, we are like patients with amnesia, living each day in a hollow and empty way without any recollection of the past and little guidance for the future. As Oscar Wilde once said, "Memory is the diary that we all carry about with us."

Like any written diary, our memory only has so many available "pages" inside it to keep a record of our experiences. To help make space in our "diary of the mind," certain memories fade over time and eventually disappear altogether, only to be replaced by new ones. Think of memory as a "work in progress." A person's memory is a lot like updating a reference book: Certain important sections will always remain the same, while less essential chapters will be revised or discarded.

The beautiful thing for marketers and brand holders about people's memories is that they aren't created inside a vacuum. People, places, things, sounds, images, and smells all blend together to create memorable experiences. This is why the designers of cult brands focus so hard on constantly creating experiential environments to stimulate our senses. Create enough of an incredible sensory experience for your customer, and not only the experience—but also your brand's product—will embed itself in that person's memory.

One more time: Create lasting memories for your customers, and your brand will have an exponentially greater chance of being the consumer's brand of choice. Your competitor will have no chance. Remember: Emotional connections are hard to break. All the marketing in the world can't trump the power of enjoyable memories in the human mind. When you create memorable experiences for your customers, you "seed" future brand loyalty. After all, who doesn't enjoy reliving memorable experiences whenever they have the chance?

 Designers of cult brands understand that we not only cherish memories, we also use them to help shape who we are as individuals. How we act, how we look, what we wear, and what we ultimately buy all relate to past experience. Does your brand create memorable experiences for its customers?

Keep Your Brand-Memory Connections Consistent

Because "the diary of the mind" is constantly being rewritten, some old memories fade and new ones take their place. This is important to realize, because it means that the warmth and good feelings a customer may once have had for a brand *because it was connected to an enjoyable memory* run the risk of fading and disappearing over time. As this positive "brand-memory connection" fades and disappears, the enhanced loyalty and fondness your customer had for your product or service typically fades and disappears, too.

The good news is that smart cult brand makers know how to counteract the loss of past memories and preserve the powerful *brand-memory connection* that they enjoy with their customers. For starters, the people behind cult brands are pillars of consistency. They work hard to stay visible to their customers with the same message day after day, year after year. Cult brander Jimmy Buffett is a prime example of consistency in action. While most recording artists go on tour only when they have a new album to promote, Buffett has toured every summer for decades. And he continues to crank out a new album almost on a yearly basis.

Even the most devoted Buffett fans seem to realize that Buffett's consistency is an essential part of his lasting power and appeal. "Parrot Heads have continued to stay strong in number over the years because Jimmy continues to tour every year," explains Jim Ugi, the founder of BuffettNews.com, a popular Web site for Buffett fans.[3]

Oprah Winfrey and Star Trek follow the consistency formula as well. For over fifteen years now, Oprah Winfrey has cranked out on a nearly daily basis a new edition of the *Oprah Winfrey*

Show, while Paramount has produced five different *Star Trek* television series and nine motion pictures over the past thirty-five years. The underlying values and message that *Star Trek* and Oprah deliver to their fans through these shows and movies have remained consistent. Both Oprah and *Star Trek* remain too visible for their followers to "forget about" them.

Don't Forget the Value of Nostalgia

Brands that already have a rich brand history and strong *brand-memory connections* should strongly consider using nostalgia as a weapon in their customer loyalty arsenal. Memories for your brand simply can't fade or disappear when your product or service constantly reminds your customers of favorable past experiences they've had. People are inherently nostalgic creatures who love to relive enjoyable past experiences whenever they have the chance. Just look at how cult brander Volkswagen proved this idea beautifully when it successfully launched the New Beetle in 1998.

As Steve Keys, Volkswagen of America's Director of Corporate Communications recalls, "There were a lot of emotions tied up with the original Beetle, and we felt the New Beetle was a great opportunity to rekindle some of these emotions and interest in Volkswagen."[4]

Keep in mind that the New Beetle shares *none* of the mechanical parts of the original Beetle and comes with many convenience features consumers now expect in cars, like power locks, power windows, and anti-lock brakes. Yet Volkswagen's designers went out of their way to keep much of the original Beetle's funky shape and styling. Volkswagen even preserved within the New Beetle those important interior stylistic details of the original Bug, including the signature flower vase in the dashboard. The end result was a new car wrapped around powerful old memories.

Beetle fanatics are well aware they are buying a "new car with old memories" when they purchase a New Beetle. Explains *Bug Tales* coauthor and Beetle lover Paul Klebahn, "The reason why this car has ended up being so popular is that it reminded people about their past."[5] Smartly, VW further rekindled the strong *brand-memory connections* the car enjoyed by launching a New Beetle ad campaign that included nostalgia-heavy slogans like "More Power, Less Flower" and "Its Engine's in the Front, But Its Heart's in the Same Place."

The nostalgia push worked. Spurred by strong first-year sales, in 1998 Volkswagen reported its best annual sales results in North America in seventeen years.[6] Best of all, the excitement and buzz surrounding the New Beetle brought a new wave of customers into VW dealerships, many of whom hadn't considered owning a Volkswagen in years. Nostalgia is power. It rekindles old memories and helps create new ones. So, does your company have a rich brand heritage just waiting to be rediscovered? Your customers yearn for the past. Give it to them.

 The powerful *brand-memory connections* you've created with your customers–and the ensuing brand loyalty customers have given you in return–don't have to fade or disappear over time. Cult brands stay fresh in the "diary of the mind" when marketing stresses consistency and nostalgia.

The Competitive Human Spirit

The need for competition lies at the heart of the human spirit. We are a species that loves to compete. We thrive on it. Many of us can't get enough of it. Just look at all those Olympians killing themselves to win gold medals and all those brainy kids going for that 4.0 grade point average. They are only a small sample of the competitive spirit in action.

Choose any profession, and you'll find it filled with individuals who want to be the best at what they do. You, for example, probably wouldn't be reading this book unless you want to become the absolute *best* marketer for your brand. True, some of us are more competitive than others. And absolutely *no one* enjoys losing. You don't have to be legendary Green Bay Packers football coach Vince Lombardi to know that victory is always sweeter than defeat.

For competition to exist there must be a worthy opponent and adversary to battle against who wants to achieve the same goal or win the same prize. Competition can't exist if there is no opposing force to duel against. Many of us live for such competition. What fun is a football game if the visiting team doesn't show up? Or, who would go see a race with only one runner? What about a chili cooking contest with only one entrant? Coke without Pepsi? McDonald's without Burger King? Talk about a boring and bland world. Rivalries fill our need to be challenged and pushed to the limit.

Competition also breeds strength and unity. Want to quickly bring a group of people together around a common cause and energize them? Create or find an archenemy, some group, organization, company, or person that directly conflicts with their own belief system, goals, feelings, or dreams. Then get out of the way and watch the sparks fly. Consider the race to put the first man on the moon back in the sixties. Would President Kennedy, NASA, and the American people have been nearly as energized if our Cold War nemesis, the Soviet Union, wasn't also hard at work on the same goal? Of course not!

Having a fierce competitor or opposing force is at the very *core* of promoting a successful cult brand. In fact, both the makers and followers of cult brands love a Yin-Yang relationship with some opposing force in the marketplace. You and your rival need each other to stay strong and energized. It's hardly a coincidence that *all* of the nine cult brands in this book have historically had very clear and very visible archenemies or nemeses.

 As human beings, we thirst for competition and the opportunity to be the best. The vast majority of us enjoy having rivalries in sports, life, and business. Rivals push us. They make us work harder and reach deeper into our psyches in our quest to be number one. Who's your brand's rival?

Every Cult Brand Has Enemies

Cult expert and thought-reform consultant Jerry Whitfield goes as far as to say that he believes "every cult will have its enemies."[7] Whitfield is speaking primarily of destructive personality cults with extremist leaders like Jim Jones and David Koresh. He is not referring to cult brands. However, his point is also relevant in the world of marketing and cult branding. Cult brands' "archenemies" are not necessarily living and breathing individuals, companies, or organizations. Your cult brand's archenemy can just as easily be an opposing set of views, ideals, philosophies, or even that age-old nemesis, the status quo.

For instance, Oprah's archenemy really isn't Jerry Springer or another low-brow talk-show host. Her brand's mission is to provide self-empowerment and self-improvement in the daily lives of her viewers, and she is essentially dedicated to defeating individuals or groups that attempt to block her ideological path. Get in the way of Oprah's mission and risk feeling her wrath. In 1996, one such "anti-Oprah" force emerged in the form of a group of Texas cattlemen after the *Oprah Winfrey Show* ran a program questioning if U.S. beef was safe for consumption and free from "mad cow disease."

While this particular show received widespread support from Oprah's viewers, it got loud criticism from the beef industry, which quickly drew up a high-profile, $12-million libel suit against Winfrey. While Oprah may not have enjoyed the legal battle that ensued, she quickly took advantage of the situation, airing her show for weeks from Amarillo, Texas, where the trial was held. Clearly, the threat of "the cattlemen" energized Oprah's followers to new levels. In fact, one group of Oprah fans even went so far as to stage a protest rally that included trampling raw hamburgers underfoot in a show of solidarity![8] The gratifying payoff came when Oprah won the lawsuit.

Obviously, Linux followers don't walk to the same drum beat as Oprah's fans, but the open-source advocates clearly feel they are in an ideological war as well. It isn't as easy as saying that

Microsoft or Bill Gates are Linux's archenemies. The battle lines are much broader. Essentially, in one corner stands Linux and its proponents, all individuals who are dedicated to empowering software developers and building the best operating system possible. In the other corner Linux followers place all monopolistic corporations that they feel make "crummy software."

Perhaps Linux evangelist Eric Raymond best summed up the "Linux cause" and what the open-source community views as its true archenemies when he told a *Washington Post* reporter in 1998, "Open source is a way to give power to individuals and deny coercive power to the government and monopolistic corporations."[9]

Unquestionably, Microsoft has played right into the Linux movement's hands and become over the past few years the clearest and most visible representation of "the dark side." A notable example of this behavior came in 2001, when Microsoft CEO Steve Ballmer told the *Chicago Sun-Times* that "Linux is a cancer."[10] These types of public comments from the world's largest software company about Linux have only furthered the fervor and resolve of many open-source devotees. Every revolution needs a villain, and Microsoft's critical public comments have only helped unify and galvanize the Linux brand.

 Followers of Oprah Winfrey and Linux both believe they are fighting ideological crusades against dark opposing forces. So, do your brand's ideals and values clash with any visible—and perhaps larger—competitors in your market? Identify a "Dark Side." Then go battle it!

Apple's Battle Against the "Evil Force," Microsoft • Linux isn't the only cult brand that effectively uses Microsoft and Bill Gates as living symbols of "ignorance" and "inferiority" to help rally its followers. Even though Microsoft is one of the largest developers of software for the Mac, Apple has relished painting Bill Gates' company as being uncreative, uninventive, super-controlling, and ultra-corporate or, in a phrase: "the anti-Apple personified." For Apple, this bold positioning strategy continues to work. By painting the two extremes, Apple helps solidify in Mac followers' minds how decidedly "different" and unique Apple is from any other computer company, particularly the "bad guy," Microsoft.

This "anti-card" can be an extremely powerful strategy for any company to play. "You can definitely establish your brand by what you're not, such as anti-IBM and anti-conformity," according to Christopher Escher, Apple's former VP of Corporate Communications and now the VP of Marketing for Responsys, a marketing company.[11] While this argument certainly makes sense, it's probably hard for someone who is not a Mac fanatic to understand why Apple continues to swim against the gigantic Windows tsunami. Are these people crazy?

Hardly. Laugh if you like, but many Mac users genuinely feel persecuted. Historically, persecuted communities unify and stick together and rarely fold under pressure. Remember, customers of cult brands have a need for self-actualization and the fulfillment of dreams and passions and often don't want acceptance and assimilation into the mainstream. In many ways, the more Microsoft has come to dominate the computing landscape over the past decade, the more Apple's core user base has united. In fact, one almost gets the sense that hard-core Mac users relish being in the minority.

"Since you now have nine out of ten people using PCs and sneering at you, Mac users have been driven into their own Macintosh ghetto where they hang together like a brotherhood," explains Michael Tchong, a marketing expert and founder of *MacWEEK* magazine.[12]

Apple Computer has always liked having an archenemy so its followers can crusade against it. In fact, when the company looked to be on the verge of extinction in the mid-nineties, it brought back charismatic former Apple employee Guy Kawasaki as its "Chief Evangelist" with his main job being to revitalize the Mac faithful.

Kawasaki wasted little time in frequently and vividly portraying Microsoft Corporation and Bill Gates as being a giant, slow-moving provider of inferior and restrictive software. Not surprisingly, Kawasaki's bold and inventive rallying cry, "Save computer users from the Gates of Hell," quickly became widely adopted and revered by the freethinking Mac faithful.[13] The Mac nation now had a new head cheerleader to help formulate and direct their feelings of anger and nonconformity.

In addition to traveling the country giving speeches and meeting with Mac users, Kawasaki also set up a pro-Mac on-line newsletter called the EvangeList. Known simply as "The List" among Mac users, it featured positive stories about how people were using their Macs, as well as occasional attacks by Kawasaki against Microsoft and seemingly "pro-Microsoft" writers in the media. By the time Kawasaki had again left his position as Apple's chief evangelist in late 1998, the EvangeList had grown to over 40,000 subscribers, and Apple was back on firm ground with the successful launch of its new iMac computer line and the return of Apple founder Steve Jobs as CEO.[14]

Would Apple have survived in the mid-nineties without Kawasaki and his small band of anti-Microsoft evangelists? Probably. But having a visible archenemy unquestionably made the revitalization of the Apple brand that much easier. Kawasaki still believes today that identifying and positioning Microsoft as a visible "Apple enemy" in the mid-nineties was valuable to his cause. "It certainly was a point of strength and unity," says Kawasaki. "Every cult needs a 'grand opposition' that it can fight on ideological terms, not mundane parameters such as market share."[15]

 Cult brands like comic book superheroes often have archenemies. Superman always fought Lex Luther, and Batman had the Joker. Look at your own brand for a second. Is there a "grand opposition" that you can face and rally against?

Does a Cult Brand Need an Archenemy?

During the mid-eighties and throughout the 1990s, WWE constantly battled against its bitter rival, World Championship Wrestling, for TV ratings, fans, and wrestling talent. Even though WWE regularly body slammed the WCW on all three of these fronts, WWE was able to unify and energize its fans and employees for years by selling itself as the "scrappy underdog" in this rivalry. After all, WCW was owned by Turner

Broadcasting, the giant cable TV network headed by the illustrious Ted Turner with far more financial firepower than the independent WWE, or so the thinking always went.

It was the kind of match-up of opposing forces that wrestling fans just couldn't get enough of. Talk to veteran fans, and you'll quickly find out that they threw their allegiance to one of these two companies, but rarely both. Not surprisingly, fans of WCW and WWE scrappily debated for years about which company's wrestlers were better, tougher, cooler—you name it. This rivalry only heated up further in the mid-nineties when WCW actually leapt WWE in the TV ratings for a period of time after it began featuring former legendary WWE superstars like Hulk Hogan.

While this rivalry may seem downright childish and even bizarre to a nonwrestling fan who is not into "sports entertainment," the bottom line is that the rivalry undoubtedly helped create excitement and sell more tickets. After all, what WWE or WCW fan *didn't* want to tune in each night and see their favorite wrestlers trash talk about the rival company or find out that one of their superstars had just been "stolen" by the other company? An added bonus to the long-running WCW-WWE rivalry was that Vince McMahon and Ted Turner made no bones about the fact that they both genuinely disliked each other.

This long-running feud took a dramatic turn in March of 2001 when the McMahons proudly announced in a surprise move that WWE had acquired the ailing and unprofitable WCW for an undisclosed price.[16] Bye-bye WCW. By making this deal, for the first time in its history WWE no longer had an archenemy of any real significance. While WWE has promised to keep the WCW brand alive in some form, it essentially now has a monopoly on pro wrestling. Will this acquisition prove to be a good thing for WWE brand long term?

"I think the fans and the offices of the wrestling companies fed off the competition. It really added to the drama of the shows when these rivalries were incorporated into the storylines," explains wrestling expert and consultant Court Bauer. "Talent was constantly being fought over between WWE and WCW, which the fans loved. Now they have nothing like that."[17]

So far, WWE's management seems excited (understandably so) and not concerned in the least that it no longer faces a rival of any real significance, even though the TV ratings have noticeably fallen over the past two years. Sales are also off their record highs. In addition, some wrestling critics now claim that the storylines of WWE's matches and shows have become stale, tired, and predictable since the WCW purchase. In short, while WWE is still a dynamite cult brand, this is a firm now without clear sailing in its future.

Professional wrestling is a business that traditionally goes through up-and-down cycles of popularity. WWE's recent slowdown in TV ratings and overall business may not be due to the fact that it recently eliminated its core rival. However, it's very plain that archenemies are a core component of every successful cult brand. Again, *every* revolution must have its villain. So, ask yourself: Has your brand's archenemy started to fade or even disappear? Don't celebrate. It may sound counterintuitive, but it may be time to find a *new* nemesis for your followers!

Find a revolution throughout history that didn't have a villain. Do you know of one? Cult brands and their followers need villains. What is your brand fighting against and for? Surely, there must be some dark opposing force in your brand's path!

Conclusion

Putting the Seven Golden Rules to Work in Your Own Business

CHANCES ARE that if you're like us, the first thing you do when you pick up a new business book is to immediately flip to the last chapter and skim through it. Some people call this a bad habit. Not us. We read the last chapter first because it saves time and let's us determine if the rest of the book will be worthwhile and useful. Plus, authors often save the best for last. With readers like ourselves in mind, in this last chapter we take all the ideas from the earlier chapters and compress them into a couple of short, easily digestible pages. If you've read this book from beginning to end (and we appreciate that!), we think you'll find this last chapter highly useful and valuable.

Let's take our seven common characteristics that virtually all cult brands share and break each one down to its very essence. Only the key points, no fluff or fancy MBA-speak. Think of this section as your own cult-branding notebook and workbook rolled into one.

Marketers, business owners, entrepreneurs, and managers who are serious about building cult-branding battle plans absolutely must have a thorough understanding and grasp of the Seven Golden Rules of Cult Branding. The questions interspersed throughout this chapter not only summarize the key elements of cult branding, they give you a readily available plan for putting them to work in your own business. We want to see all of our readers succeed.

So, read this section, answer the questions, use the Golden Rules with your own brand, and let us know your results!

Summary of the Seven Golden Rules of Cult Branding

1. Consumers Want to Be Part of a Group That's Different

We are a society that is addicted to communication. Computers and e-mail. Cell phones and land-line phones. Fax machines. Handheld PDAs and interactive two-way pagers. Twenty-four-hour cable news channels. How and why do we use all these different communication devices? Primarily to form and maintain distinct social groups, since as human beings, we are all inherently social animals with a constant need to interact and socialize with others. Perhaps most important, we not only want to be part of groups made up of like-minded individuals, we all enjoy being different and standing out from the rest of "the pack" in an increasingly cookie-cutter world.

A. How is your company's product or service already different from the competition? List how your brand is noticeably different.

_____

_____

_____

_____

B. What are some ways you can make your product or service stand out even more from the rest of the marketplace? List them.

_____

_____

_____

_____

C. Okay. Now it's time to make your brand not just different but insanely different. List your craziest ideas for product differentiation.

_____

_____

_____

_____

2. Cult Brand Inventors Show Daring and Determination

Cult branders are like famous inventors and explorers. Even in the face of doubters and critics, they hold the courage and determination needed to dare to be different and succeed. Cult branders believe in themselves and their products and services. They not only challenge conventional wisdom, they try to shatter it whenever they get the chance. You must be willing to take significant risks to really make your brand stand out in the marketplace and attract a cadre of loyal followers. The people behind cult brands are fighters and leaders. They are not quitters or followers. Never fear failure. That which does not kill a cult brand makes it stronger.

A. With big risks often come big rewards. What is the biggest branding-related risk your company has taken in its history? In the past year?

_____

_____

_____

_____

B. What's a marketing idea that your company decided was too risky to pursue? Write it down. Does it challenge conventional wisdom?

_____

_____

_____

_____

C. That which does not kill a cult brand makes it stronger. Write down your brand's marketing failures. Be honest. Learn from them.

_____

_____

_____

_____

3. Cult Brands Sell Lifestyles

Cult brands are just plain fun. Their products and services always put smiles on their customers' faces and make them feel better about themselves. Not only do cult brands provide their followers with a temporary escape from life's responsibilities, they help them fulfill their passions and dreams. In other words, cult branders capitalize on our human need for greater feelings of self-actualization by developing products and services that help fulfill high-level needs. A company with a cult brand doesn't just sell a product or a service. These companies develop and sell "the tools" that allow the followers of their brands to pursue their dreams and celebrate distinct new lifestyles.

A. Is your brand fun? Does it make your customers happy and make them feel good about themselves? List everything that's fun about your brand.

_____

_____

_____

_____

B. What are the passions and dreams of your customers? List them below. How can your brand help fulfill these wants?

_____

_____

_____

_____

C. Followers of cult brands are buying into a lifestyle—not just a product or a service. What is the lifestyle your customers are really seeking?

_____

_____

_____

_____

4. Listen to the Choir and Create Cult Brand Evangelists!

Cult brands always focus on serving the wants and needs of the customers they already have. Cult brands don't get sucked into the trap of building products and services that hypothetically might attract new customers. Look at the congregation of customers your brand already has. Respect your choir. Value their opinions. Reward them. Listen to them. Never ignore an enthusiastic follower of your brand. Remember that core followers all want to believe, but first they need to see miracles in the form of unexpected gifts and surprises. Do extraordinary things for your choir, and they'll become incredible brand evangelists.

A. Does your company really listen to the feedback and suggestions of its most loyal followers? What are they saying? Write their opinions below.

_____

_____

_____

_____

B. Customers want to be appreciated. They want their suggestions to be heard and used. How do you reward your best customers?

_____

_____

_____

_____

C. Every company can do more to show its customers it appreciates them. What are new ways you can show your customers that you "listen?"

_____

_____

_____

_____

5. Cult Brands Always Create Customer Communities

Simply put, cult brand companies always give back. They are adamant about continually finding new ways to show their love and appreciation for the passion and devotion of their customers. Unlike seemingly faceless corporations, cult brand companies remain humble and personable. They never take their existing customers for granted. Cult brand companies build strong ongoing relationships with their customers by developing and supporting customer communities. Cult brand companies aren't afraid to put aside short-term profits in favor of creating customer communities that generate powerful long-term halo effects on their business and their brand.

A. How do you communicate and stay in touch with your customers? Do you have a newsletter, a mailing list, or a fan festival?

_____

_____

_____

B. Customer communities are invaluable branding tools. What are new ways you can build a "sense of community" around your brand?

_____

_____

_____

C. Cult brands always give back. What are some organizations and causes that your customers would love to see your brand support?

_____

_____

_____

_____

6. Cult Brands Are Inclusive

Cult brand companies are incredibly open and inclusive. They never get caught up in building imaginary profiles of ideal customers. Cult brands don't discriminate. They openly embrace everyone and anyone who is interested in their company. In fact, exclusivity isn't even in the vocabulary of the cult brander. Instead, cult brand companies welcome with open arms customers of all ages, races, creeds, and socioeconomic backgrounds. Cult brand companies prove to their customers that they are indeed open and inclusive by helping to fulfill the deep human needs that we all share. Cult brand companies become giant support groups for like-minded individuals.

A. Is your own brand already open and inclusive—or have you focused only on targeting ideal customer segments? Why?

_____

_____

_____

_____

B. Cult brands help fulfill deep human needs that customers of all backgrounds share. What human needs can/does your brand fulfill?

_____

_____

_____

_____

C. Okay. How can you take the human needs you just identified and make them even more intertwined and visible within your brand?

_____

_____

_____

_____

7. **Cult Brands Promote Personal Freedom and Draw Power from Their Enemies**

It goes without saying that no one likes to feel owned or controlled. As human beings, we all cherish our freedom. Knowing this, cult brand companies all promote underlying themes of freedom and nonconformity. To help cement these feelings of freedom and develop lasting brand loyalty, cult brand companies work hard to create memorable sensory experiences for their customers. In addition, they stay fresh in the "diary of the mind" with brand consistency and nostalgia marketing. Finally, all cult brand companies draw strength and unity from identifying and targeting an archenemy—an opposing brand, person, or group—that conflicts with the cult brand company's values/goals.

A. Does your company's brand provide your customers with feelings of freedom and liberation from "the system?" How? List your thoughts here.

_____

_____

_____

_____

B. Is your brand experience consistent? Do you take advantage of your brand's nostalgia? How can you improve in both these areas?

_____

_____

_____

_____

Well, that's it! Your official crash course on the Seven Golden Rules of Cult Branding is finished. You and your company are now ready to start cult branding with the best of them! However, before we go, we have one last request.

If you haven't already done so, take a few minutes and go back and write down your answers to the questions in this chapter. While we're not going to tell you that by answering the questions you'll come up with at least one new million-dollar marketing idea, we've seen some very interesting things happen when people are forced to put their thoughts down on paper. You've already come this far. Why not go the distance?

As we've already said, we believe that the only business books worth their salt are the ones with readily understood ideas that we can actually go out and use. We hope this book succeeds in providing you with digestible bites of cult-branding tips, tactics, suggestions, and advice. If only one sentence in this book helps spark a "brand" new idea or line of thinking that you can implement in your business, then it has succeeded and was worth "the price of admission."

Writing this book has been tremendous fun for both of us. Not only have we learned more about the inner workings of cult brands than we could ever have imagined, but we've met many truly unique and interesting people in the process. We feel incredibly lucky to have been given this opportunity, and we're absolutely convinced that cult branding is going to explode in popularity and usage through the marketing world over the course of the next decade as more companies get serious about brand loyalty.

Finally, don't hesitate to contact us. E-mail us. Call us. Send us smoke signals if you'd like. We'd love to hear from you. In fact, you just might make our day. Remember: We're both two hyperactive and always inquisitive marketers who are hopelessly addicted to uncovering the real secrets to effective brand building and lasting customer loyalty. We eat this stuff for breakfast, lunch, dinner, and any meals in between. Thus, we're always looking to hear cool new cult branding stories from smart marketers, entrepreneurs, business owners, and managers like yourselves. Let us know what has worked, what hasn't, and why!

Matt Ragas
matt@powerofcultbranding.com

B.J. Bueno
bjb@powerofcultbranding.com

Appendix

Interviews with Cult Experts Rick Ross
and Jerry Whitfield

I N THE COURSE of doing our research for this book, we interviewed dozens of individuals, from current and former managers and executives of our nine cult brands to many die-hard customers of cult brands. Although we learned volumes from these fascinating conversations, no two interviews had a greater influence on the customer loyalty and branding concepts we have presented in this book than our discussions with cult experts and consultants Rick Ross and Jerry Whitfield.

We had already read numerous articles and scanned a handful of books about destructive cults before speaking with either Ross or Whitfield, and we had many questions to ask. Both of these individuals were immensely helpful in explaining in simple and understandable terms how cults operate. They got to the very core of what makes cults so attractive and powerful to certain individuals. Further, both helped articulate for us the noticeable similarities and sharp differences between how cult brands and cultic groups operate, behave, and build loyalty.

We include here excerpts of our interviews with Ross and Whitfield to provide readers with the direct thoughts on cults, influence, persuasion, and branding of two real cult experts. We hope that you find this section useful and that it helps spark debate and discussion about cult branding and brand loyalty within your own organization.

Rick Ross

Cult expert and intervention specialist Rick Ross first became interested in radical groups in 1982, when his grandmother, then an eighty-three-year-old nursing home resident, was approached by an ardent cult recruiter. By working with the nursing home's management, Ross was able to put a stop to the group's aggressive recruiting in the facility. Since then, Ross has helped dozens of families rescue loved ones from the influence of destructive cults.

Ross, a consultant for both the ATF and the FBI, has been quoted in a wide range of publications, including *Newsweek*, the *Chicago Tribune*, the *Washington Post*, and the *New York Times*, and has appeared on *The Today Show*, ABC News, *Nightline*, and *Good Morning America*. He has lectured at Carnegie Mellon, Baylor University, and the University of Chicago. He lives in Jersey City, New Jersey.

RAGAS: You've performed intervention work that has helped hundreds of victims of destructive cults over the past twenty years. Based on your work, what is the profile of the average cult member?

ROSS: There is no real "average person." There are people that are more susceptible than others to cults at certain points in their life, but I think that virtually anyone is susceptible to cult recruitment. My work over the years has demonstrated this over and over again. Cult members include people from every socioeconomic background and every educational level. They essentially represent a typical cross section of the population. It is well established that at different times in our life we are more vulnerable than at other times. If you are going through a particularly difficult time in your life, if you are feeling frustrated, lonely, or depressed, you may be more likely to listen to someone from a group that claims to have answers. These groups are so deceptive in their recruitment practices that it's not clear who you are really dealing with.

RAGAS: Cult brand companies are clearly very different than destructive cults in that they are very open and honest about their brand's mission and purpose. They also all have a sense of family around their brand.

ROSS: In a very broad and general sense, I think that everyone is looking for a sense of inclusion and belonging. Particularly, we want this in a society that is very often overwhelming. These groups offer simple and direct explanations for virtually everything. There are no loose ends. That can be comforting. In a society where there is a very significant divorce rate and where families are frequently fragmented, these cults represent a sense of family and inclusion. People often are attracted to that. Some people that participate in cult groups may have a background of low self-esteem. By becoming part of a group and identifying with that group identity they lift themselves up from these feelings of low self-esteem to feelings of elitism and being in the vanguard of some spiritual, religious, or political movement. This gives them a lift emotionally. That may parallel someone who is disadvantaged and feels marginalized by society, but by wearing "x brand" or by participating in "x product" they have an altered identity that makes them feel better about themselves and makes their self-image improve.

RAGAS: Our research has shown without a doubt that cult brands are all focused on making their followers feel better about themselves. From Star Trek to Parrot Heads, we've found that this is the same.

ROSS: I often use Star Trek fans as examples of a benign cult. At the other extreme are destructive cults, which I define as groups with an absolute authoritarian figure at the top of a pyramid scheme of authority in which there is virtually no accountability for that leader. People abdicate their ability to make their own value judgments. They largely abdicate their critical thinking and then relegate that to the leader. The group is essentially focused on that personality and driven by that personality. The ultimate end of it would be that the leader or small cadre of leaders exploits the membership by either hurting or harming them, which could be sexual, financial, physical or psychological and emotional.

RAGAS: Can you tell us some of the distinct differences between destructive cults, which you've just outlined for us, and harmless and benign cults, which we characterize as cult brands in our book?

ROSS: I'm going to draw a bright line between a destructive cult and a benign cult, such as Trekkers. Many cults—in fact most cults—may be benign in the sense of there being a cult following for a particular person, product, place, or thing of some sort. I think that with many of these groups, such as die-hard Elvis fans hanging out at Graceland, that becoming a member of those cult followings is kind of like receiving a license to be weird. You go out and find your kindred spirits—other people that would like to "be weird" also—and then you can be weird together and basically feel weird no more! By and large, I find that most people into things like New Age, UFO theorists, Trekkers, Elvis fans, or avid Barbie doll collectors are basically harmless and benign. They are certainly not governed by an absolute and authoritarian figure. I'm concerned by groups that really exploit people.

RAGAS: One of the challenges we've faced with writing this book is the perception that only a certain type of person is susceptible to cult branding. People often have this "it can't happen to me" syndrome!

ROSS: When I go out and lecture at universities and colleges, the most common question audiences always ask is, what type of person joins a cult? It's their way of saying in a sense, it can't happen to me. So, one of the things I will say is, let's just call that what it is—denial! I can speak here for an hour about the brilliant students at Harvard, MIT, and Penn that were sucked in by cults, and I got them out. Now they're engineers and attorneys. One was almost a Rhodes Scholar. So stop the denial!

RAGAS: It definitely is denial. No one likes to imagine themselves being unwillingly influenced by others and falling for obvious persuasion tactics, let alone being sucked into a destructive cult!

ROSS: One of the ways you can see it is how many of you are wearing designer clothing. How many of you are wearing

Gucci or Tommy Hilfiger? How many of you bought that cologne that you have on the shelf because you really believed it would make you sexier? Or that you drive a certain car because you think it's going to "put you over." So, you yourself have been persuaded by mass marketing, advertising, propaganda, and politics. How many of you will listen more to an authority figure dressed in a dark suit with a red tie than if he were wearing a T-shirt? You yourself are susceptible to influence and persuasion techniques. Now, if you take those techniques and intensify them to the extent that these groups do twenty-four/seven with that type of persuasion, how many of you would also fall?

Jerry Whitfield

Jerry Whitfield has worked professionally in the cult field since 1989 as an intervention specialist. He and his wife, Hana, both became dedicated to helping individuals break away from destructive cults when they left the Church of Scientology after a combined thirty years as members. Over the past decade, this husband-and-wife duo has helped over one hundred families rescue family members and loved ones that were trapped inside destructive cults.

The Whitfields have done countless interviews over the past decade for radio, TV, newspapers, and magazines. They have appeared on *Larry King Live* and *Sally Jessie Rafael,* as well as *60 Minutes* both in the U.S. and Australia. Tireless in their mission, the Whitfields have traveled throughout North America, Europe, Africa, and Australia to help families in need and perform interventions. The couple lives in Cape Coral, Florida.

RAGAS: Everyone seems to have their own definition of what qualifies a group as a cult, but what are some of the common characteristics you have found through your work that cults have?

WHITFIELD: If you look in the dictionary, it gives you a good definition of a cult, but it's so broad that Mother Theresa could be considered a cult. But what makes one group a cult and keeps another from becoming a cult even if they espouse exactly the same beliefs is the politics of the group. Where is the center of control? Who is controlling whom? I would certainly consider the Taliban and Osama bin Laden to be very cultish since they convinced this group of people to get into airplanes, die for Allah, and kill 5,000 people they don't know, that they've never met, and who aren't doing anything to them. How could you get someone to do something like that?

RAGAS: Yes, how do cults get people to do unthinkable and horrendous things like that? What are the tools and tactics that they use to gain so much control and influence over a person's life?

WHITFIELD: Well, how does Madison Avenue or Fifth Avenue get us to buy things? Let's say you want to buy a sports car. What do you think of with a sports car? Well, you think of sexy women. So sports cars have sex appeal. A big luxurious sports car has lots of sex appeal. Or, how did Hitler do what he did? One of the things that Hitler wanted to do was to get rid of the vermin in society so he cleaned up the cities and got rid of the rats. After he did this, he told the nation that the Jews were the social pestilence—the social rats—and that they should be gotten rid of also. By that time, people had already developed this big hatred for rats so he positioned the Jews as equivalent to the rats. That's positioning and thought reform.

RAGAS: There are a lot of misconceptions out in our society right now about the profile of the typical cult member. Most of the time, we automatically think of cult members as poorly educated and not very intelligent people, but that generally isn't the truth, is it?

WHITFIELD: The general profile of a cult member is a person who has above average intelligence, is open and honest with other people, and who anticipates that people will be open and honest back to them. This person has the ability to think in abstract ideas and is probably altruistic. They want to help change things. They want to improve their life and the lives of others. That probably describes almost every fire fighter in the world.

RAGAS: It not only describes probably every fire fighter in the world, but also a large chunk of the entire population. Friends, family members, neighbors, colleagues—you name it! Let's get back to talking about why cults have so much power over their members.

WHITFIELD: Okay. What is it that cults are giving people so that they are willing to give up their better judgment? I can only surmise. I think there is an emotional need that is being met that the cult provides that is above and beyond what this person is getting from society, yet this person needs it. I think that cults probably encompass a number of different needs that are different for each person. Most cults give you recognition. They make you feel special. They tell you you're one of the special people because you're "one of us." And most cults will also give you a sense of family.

RAGAS: Let's talk about cult recruiting tactics. Our research has shown that there is a big difference about how cult brands and destructive cults go about recruiting new customers and followers.

WHITFIELD: I think there is a huge difference in the recruiting tactics of groups like Parrot Heads and Trekkers as opposed to destructive cults—what we call high-demand groups. The recruiting for cults is deceptive, whereas if you want to become a Trekker, you can get on the Web and find out everything you want to know. If you want to become a Harley-Davidson fan, you can go buy books, look on the Web, talk to people, and find out everything you want to know about Harley-Davidson. But when you want to join a cult, you are spoon-fed the information. When "you're ready for it," you get the next level of information. And as you get higher levels of information, you find out how much more important you've become, because you're more special than everyone below you. Not until you've proven yourself on the step you're on are you allowed to get to the next level of information.

RAGAS: We can't speak about how destructive cults operate, but we have found through our research for this book that cult brands constantly focus on making their members feel special and appreciated. How do destructive cults accomplish this same task?

WHITFIELD: They tell you! In Scientology, they tell you that only we have the technology to save the world. And there are a lot of Christians who believe that if you're not a Christian then you're not going to go to heaven; you're going to go to hell. God gave his only begotten Son, and those who believe will have everlasting life. Cults all have words of significance that go along with this thinking. In Scientology, you can become "clear." In the Marines, you can become a corporal or a sergeant. You get hash marks on your sleeve. In the Army, if you get your Ranger insignia you get a beret. There are all sorts of ways that cults can accomplish this same thing whether it's with a pin, words, levels of classification, years of experience, or something like officer or non-officer status.

Notes

Introduction

1. Rick Ross, interview by authors. Fall 2001.
2. Stacy J. Willis, "Arrival of Cult Specialist in Las Vegas Stirs Debate," *Las Vegas Sun*, August 24, 2001.
3. Margaret Singer, *Cults in Our Midst* (San Francisco: Jossey-Bass Publishers, 1995), p. 17.
4. Jerry Whitfield, interview by authors. Fall 2001.
5. Margaret Singer, *Cults in Our Midst* (San Francisco: Jossey-Bass Publishers, 1995), p. 19.
6. Abraham H. Maslow, *The Maslow Business Reader* (New York: John Wiley & Sons, 2000), p. 1.
7. Ibid., p. 3.
8. Oprah.com—Fact Sheet (www.oprah.com/about/press/about_press_owsfaq.jhtml).
9. Patricia Sellers, "The Business of Being Oprah," *Fortune*, April 1, 2002, pp. 50–64.

10. Valerie Kuklenski, "The Story of O—Winfrey's Devotees Seeking Life's Truths," *Los Angeles Daily News,* July 1, 2000.

11. Richard Truett, "Beetle-Mania Hits the Streets," *The Orlando Sentinel,* March 19, 1998.

12. Wanda Jankowski, "Star Trek: Beaming Up Sales for 30 Years," *Gifts & Decorative Accessories,* June 1, 1996, p. 130.

13. WWFECorpBiz.com—Media Facts (www.wwfecorpbiz.com/).

14. Eric Pooley, "Still Rockin' in Jimmy Buffett's Margaritavile," *Time,* August 17, 1998.

15. Yahoo! Finance—Vans Inc. News (http://biz.yahoo.com/n/v/Vans.html).

16. May Wong, "Windows Won War, but Apple Led Way," *Associated Press,* August 12, 2001.

17. Hoovers.com—Apple Computer, Inc. (http://biz.yahoo.com/n/v/Vans.html).

18. Amy Harmon, "Rebel with a Cause: Challenge to Microsoft Windows Comes from Parallel Silicon Universe," *Seattle Post-Intelligencer,* June 13, 1999.

19. CNET News.com staff, "Linux Making Corporate Inroads," *CNET News.com,* August 15, 2001.

20. James P. Miller, "Harley Hits a Rough Patch?," *CNN.com,* February 5, 2001.

21. Anita Lienert, "A Limited-Edition Hog: Ford Pickup Taps into Harley Image," *The Detroit News,* August 23, 2000.

22. Jonathan Fahey, "Love into Money," *Forbes,* January 7, 2002, pp. 60–65.

Rule One

1. Dan Madsen, interview by authors. Fall 2001.

2. Jeff Greenwald, interview by authors. Fall 2001.

3. David Teather, "Chat Queen Oprah Shelves Her TV Book Club," *The Guardian,* April 8, 2002.

4. Debra Dickerson, "A Woman's Woman," *U.S. News & World Report,* September 29, 1997.

5. Robert Thompson, interview by authors. Fall 2001.

6. David Kirkpatrick, "Oprah Will Curtail 'Book Club' Picks," *New York Times,* April 6, 2002.

7. Glen Sanford, interview by authors. Fall 2001.

8. John Sculley, interview by authors. Fall 2001.

9. Owen Edwards, "Sects Crazed Since Its Earliest Days, Apple Has Counted on Its Cult Status for Support," *Forbes ASAP,* February 23, 1998.

10. Josh Quittner, "Apple's Latest Fruit," *Time,* January 27, 2002.

11. Paul Klebahn, interview by authors. Fall 2001.

12. James M. Flammang, *Volkswagen: Beetles, Buses & Beyond* (Iola, WI: Krause Publications, 1996), p. 78.

13. Klebahn, interview.

14. David Allen, interview by authors. Fall 2001.

15. Michelle Delio, "The Story Behind Tux the Penguin," *Wired News,* March 13, 2001.

16. Linus Torvalds and David Diamond, *Just for Fun: The Story of an Accidental Revolutionary* (New York: HarperCollins, 2001), pp. 139–140.

17. Steve Baker, "A Complete History of Tux (So Far)," www .sjbaker.org/tux.

18. Mark Humphrey, *The Jimmy Buffett Scrap Book* (New York: Citadel Press, 1993), p. 68.

19. Cindy Thompson, interview by authors. Fall 2001.

Rule Two

1. Sue Cornwell, interview by authors. Fall 2001.

2. Lou Carlozo, "It Still Flies 30 Years After Its Debut," *Chicago Tribune,* September 3, 1996.

3. Dan Madsen, interview by authors. Fall 2001.

4. Robert Strauss, "Why Is Everybody Talking?; Oprah Is Still Queen, Surrounded by Familiar Names like Phil, Ricki, and Geraldo," *Los Angeles Times,* October 1, 1995.

5. Robert Feder, interview by authors. Fall 2001.

6. Robert Thompson, interview by authors. Fall 2001.

7. Bethany McLean, "Inside the World's Weirdest Family Business," *Fortune,* October 16, 2000.

8. John Leland, "Why America's Hooked on Wrestling," *Newsweek,* February 7, 2000.

9. William Oscar Johnson, "Wrestling with Success," *Sports Illustrated,* March 25, 1991.

10. Bob Sudyk, "Vince McMahon," *The Hartford Courant,* September 5, 1999.

11. Charles Leroux, "Full Throttle," *Chicago Tribune* (Sunday Magazine), June 6, 1993.

12. Greg Field, *Harley-Davidson Evolution Motorcycles* (Osceola, WI: MBI Publishing Company, 2001), pp. 22–26.

13. Ed Carson, "Leaders and Success: Star Trek's Gene Roddenberry," *Investor's Business Daily,* November 10, 1997.

14. David Kronke, "What a Long Strange 'Trek' It's Been," *Los Angeles Times* (Calendar), September 8, 1996.

15. James M. Flammang, *Volkswagen: Beetles, Buses & Beyond* (Iola, WI: Krause Publications, 1996), pp. 32–33.

16. Eric Boehlert, "Why the XFL Tanked," *Salon.com,* May 11, 2001.

17. Linda McMahon, interview by authors. Fall 2001.

Rule Three

1. Elizabeth Corcoran, "LINUX: UNIX Power for Peanuts; Linus Torvalds and his Free Operating System," *Washington Post,* May 22, 1995.
2. Scott Nickerson, interview by authors. Fall 2001.
3. Billy Peoples, interview by authors. Fall 2001
4. Rob Malda, interview by authors. Fall 2001.
5. Stacy Peralta, interview by authors. Fall 2001.
6. Arlene Weintraub, "Vans: Chairman of the Board," *Business Week,* May 28, 2001.
7. Mike Hofman, "Upstarts: Tapping Generation Y," *Inc.,* December 1, 1999.
8. Chris Escher, interview by authors. Fall 2001.
9. Mark Leibovich, "The Spreading Grass-Roots Threat to Microsoft," *Washington Post,* December 3, 1998.
10. Thompson, interview.
11. Jeff Greenwald, interview by authors. Fall 2001.
12. Alex Salkever, "Finally, a Chance for Apple to Flourish," *Business Week Online* (Special Report: The Future of Apple), January 18, 2002.
13. Josh Quittner, "Apple's Latest Fruit," *Time,* January 27, 2002.
14. Peter Henderson, "Plugged In: Apple Sells Style, Community at New Stores," *Reuters,* October 9, 2001.
15. David Mack, "Star Trek Soars to the Final Frontier of Entertainment," *Nation's Restaurant News,* January 19, 1998.
16. Hans Greimel, "Beetle World: Volkswagen Plans Its Own Disneyland," *Salon.com,* May 31, 2000.

Rule Four

1. Lou Carlozo, "It Still Flies 30 Years after Its Debut," *Chicago Tribune,* September 3, 1996.
2. Stacy Peralta, interview by authors. Fall 2001.
3. Billy Peoples, interview by authors. Fall 2001.
4. Scott Nickerson, interview by authors. Fall 2001.
5. Apple.com—User Groups Community News (www.apple.com/usergroups/news.html).
6. Guy Kawasaki, interview by authors. Fall 2001.
7. "Driving Influences, What You Buy Can Change the Future," *Volkswagen Driver* 36, no. 2 (Fall 1998).
8. Rich Kimball, interview by authors. Fall 2001.
9. Jim Digennaro, "Generations of Innovation Summit '96," *The Late Model Bus Organization* (www.bcn.net/~limbo/summit96.html).
10. Kimball, interview.
11. Deborah D. McAdams, "Queen of the Ring (Linda McMahon of World Wrestling Federation Entertainment Inc.)," *Broadcasting & Cable,* January 8, 2001.
12. Linda McMahon, interview by authors. Fall 2001.
13. Dave Meltzer, interview by authors. Fall 2001.
14. McMahon, interview.
15. Bethany McLean, "Inside the World's Weirdest Family Business," *Fortune,* October 16, 2000.
16. Bryan Alvarez, interview by authors. Fall 2001.
17. Elizabeth Corcoran, "LINUX: UNIX Power for Peanuts; Linus Torvalds and His Free Operating System," *Washington Post,* May 22, 1995.
18. Vans.com—Company (www.Vans.com/history/hs_main.html).
19. Gary Schoenfeld, interview by authors. Fall 2001.

20. Schoenfeld, interview.

21. "Vans Acquires Vans Warped Tour for $4.1 Million," *Business Wire,* June 29, 2001.

Rule Five

1. Hayward Allen, "Sweet Ride to Success," *Corporate Report Wisconsin,* December 1, 1993.

2. Greg Field, interview by authors. Fall 2001.

3. Sam Abrahamsen, interview by authors. Fall 2001.

4. Phil Jenkins, interview by authors. Fall 2001.

5. Harley-Davidson.com—100th Anniversary (www.harley-davidson.com/EX/ANV/en/100th.asp?bmLocale=en_US).

6. Scott Maxwell, "Trekkies, " *Associated Press,* December 26, 1989.

7. Scott Nickerson, interview by authors. Fall 2001.

8. Nickerson, interview.

9. Parrot Heads in Paradise—Club Guidelines (www.phip.com/guide.cfm).

10. Mark Humphrey, *The Jimmy Buffett Scrap Book* (New York: Citadel Press, 1993), p. 164.

11. Cindy Thompson, interview by authors. Fall 2001.

12. Court Bauer, interview by authors. Fall 2001.

13. Linda McMahon, interview by authors. Fall 2001.

14. John Sculley, interview by authors. Fall 2001.

15. Sculley, interview.

16. Chris Escher, interview by authors. Fall 2001.

17. Everett Rosecrans, interview by authors. Fall 2001.

18. Rosecrans, interview.

19. Oprah.com—Oprah's Angel Network—Angel Network History (www.oprah.com/uyl/angel/uyl_angel_about.jhtml).

20. "WWF Entertainment Wraps Up Another Successful Year of Smackdown Your Vote!" World Wrestling Entertainment Inc. Press Release, October 29, 2001.

21. Apple.com—Steve Jobs' National Educational Computing Conference 2001 Keynote (www.apple.com/hotnews/articles/2001/06/necc/necc_keynote.html).

Rule Six

1. Christopher Farley, "Queen of All Media," *Time,* October 5, 1998.

2. Richard Huff, "The Power of Oprah from Beef to Books, Americans Experience a Formidable Force," *New York Daily News,* January 28, 1998.

3. Ken Ringle, "Buffett's Land of Coconut, Milk and Honey," *Washington Post,* July 26, 1998.

4. Richard Arnold, interview by authors. Fall 2001.

5. Jon Hall, interview by authors. Fall 2001.

6. Rob Malda, interview by authors. Fall 2001.

7. Stacy Peralta, interview by authors. Fall 2001.

8. Mike Hofman, "Upstarts: Tapping Generation Y," *Inc.,* December 1, 1999.

9. "Harley-Davidson: Marketing an American Icon," *@issue: The Journal of Business & Design* 2, no. 1 (1996) (www.cdf.org/cdf/atissue/vol2_1/harley/harley.html).

10. Ibid.

11. Steve Keys, interview by authors. Fall 2001.

12. "Harley-Davidson: Marketing an American Icon."

13. Michael Kiely, "Right Connections Vital to Retain Brand Loyalty," *Australian Financial Review,* March 11, 1997.

14. Jonathan Fahey, "Love into Money," *Forbes,* January 7, 2002.

Rule Seven

1. Chris Maida, interview by authors. Fall 2001.

2. Robert Young, interview by authors. Fall 2001.

3. Jim Ugi, interview by authors. Fall 2001.

4. Steve Keys, interview by authors. Fall 2001.

5. Paul Klebahn, interview by authors. Fall 2001.

6. "Volkswagen Sales in the U.S. 1998," *Automotive Intelligence* (www.autointell.com/european_companies/volkswagen/ business-figures-group/volkswag1.htm).

7. Jerry Whitfield, interview by authors. Fall 2001.

8. "Oprah Accused of Whipping up Anti-Beef Lynch Mob," *CNN.com,* January 21, 1998 (www.cnn.com/US/9801/21/oprah.beef/).

9. Mark Leibovich, "The Spreading Grass-Roots Threat to Microsoft," *Washington Post,* December 3, 1998.

10. "Microsoft CEO Takes Launch Break with the Sun-Times," *Chicago Sun-Times,* June 1, 2001.

11. Chris Escher, interview by authors. Fall 2001.

12. Michael Tchong, interview by authors. Fall 2001.

13. Jim Carlton, "Computers: Mac Evangelists Struggle to Bring Back Good Old Days," *The Wall Street Journal,* April 30, 1996.

14. Garry Barker, "Eccentric Preacher Bows Out of the Game," *Sydney Morning Herald,* April 27, 1999.

15. Guy Kawasaki, interview by authors. Fall 2001.

16. WWFECorpBiz.com—Corporate—Media (http://corporate .wwe.com).

17. Court Bauer, interview by authors. Fall 2001.

Index

Are you an aspiring **CULT Brander?**

Then we want to hear from you. Cult branders unite!

www.powerofcultbranding.com

Matthew W. Ragas • **Bolivar J. Bueno**
Cult Branding Strategy
Consulting • Speaking • Training

matt@powerofcultbranding.com
bjb@powerofcultbranding.com

toll free: (877) 246-4591 / fax: (208) 275-7280